ADORNMENT

The Complete Guide to
Jewelry Sales

Carson Gibbs

DEDICATION

To the OG team. This is for you guys.

CONTENTS

ACKNOWLEDGMENTS

I want to give a huge shoutout to my wife who has supported me throughout this entire process. This book would not have been possible without her.

Secondly, I would like to acknowledge all my mentors and leaders who are always pushing me to become better each day. Thank you.

CHAPTER 1: INTRODUCTION

If you want to succeed you should strike out on new paths, rather than travel the worn paths of accepted success.
John D. Rockefeller

If you have ever suspected that your competition knew something that you didn't, you're probably right. Successful sales professionals don't owe their greatness to luck. They're on top because they know more about their products than the competition and they execute sales techniques better.

Whether you're just beginning or you have previous experience, this book is going to help you swiftly increase your knowledge and professionalism as a jeweler. All the knowledge you will gain from this book will help you acquire wealth, increase your God given sales skills, and improve your diamond presentations.

Giving a diamond is among the ultimate gestures of love and commitment. At the same time, fine diamond jewelry also represents a significant investment for most people. Consumers now have access to the largest treasure trove of information in the history of the world. However, buying a diamond is one of the biggest "blind" purchases they will ever make – one the customer knows little or nothing about. Think about that for a second. People are willing to spend thousands of their hard-earned dollars on something they may not fully understand or appreciate.

Most diamond customers are smart enough to do some research on that treasure trove of an internet before walking in your doors. However, a search for diamonds on Google will bring up more than two billion possible websites. As a result, today's diamond customers can be overwhelmed and not understand which facts are important and which are trivial. They need help and guidance from an informed sales professional. Even more, they need to trust the help and guidance they receive.

By committing to learning the sales fundamentals throughout this book, you are going to be able to provide your customers with the confidence to trust you and to trust the diamond industry while leaving you with a hefty commission that you have earned through hard work. You are taking an important step in your career. You're going to increase your knowledge, build your confidence, and gain the skills you need to professionally sell diamond jewelry effectively.

You are a member of an industry that touches all corners of the globe and is as old as human existence itself. More than 100,000 years ago, our primitive ancestors discovered beautiful seashells, shiny crystals and other objects that filled them with a sense of wonder. What they didn't keep they traded for other objects of equal wonderment and some precious stones even gained spiritual identities, powers and curses. Today the global gem and jewelry industry is connected by millions of people who are filled with that same ancient wonderment.

Some mine these precious materials from the Earth while others mold these materials into artistic expressions to dazzle and express what we cannot say with mere words alone. Lastly, there are those like you and I who have the opportunity to meet those who are in search of that great beauty, value, and meaning.

We are the lucky ones. We get to meet individuals from all walks of life who have some emotion they wish to express to another. We get to help them discover new and unique ways to communicate those emotions by presenting them with pieces of jewelry as deeply rooted in love as they are. We are lucky because we have the freedom to become as successful as we would like to be. In this profession no one limits your income but you. There are no income ceilings. There is only a lack of effort that will hold you back. So why don't more people do it? Because selling jewelry isn't easy.

But you have this book. You are willing to work harder and learn. You proved that when you decided to be vulnerable enough to seek additional help and you are now taking the time out of your busy life to read up on your profession. You are going to close more sales, get more 5-star reviews and make more money by practicing what this book has to offer.

With all of that in mind, remember this - you can't just sit in a chair and tell yourself that you will absorb all the things that are tucked within these pages. You must be willing to go out and try them for yourself. Take what you have read and craft it into your own words. If you believe that there are better ways of saying things or better questions to ask when you add your own unique spin on them. You will be more successful by being yourself.

This book is a framework of techniques, methods and

knowledge that are meant to enhance your sales creativity. Each product you sell, person you meet and diamond you show is going to be unique in their own special way. At times you may wish that was a simple 6 step process for jewelry selling success, but if it was that easy than anyone could do it. You should be proud that you are seeking to become a jeweler of the highest caliber. Take these teachings and make them your own. Stamp them with your own individual ideas, emotions, and skills. Do this while learning all there is to know and you will soar higher than you have ever imagined.

You should also notice that the chapters are arranged in such a way that in the beginning we will be looking at the very foundation of the jewelry world before we move on to the sales techniques and tools themselves. There is a logic to the madness. Think of the analogy: if you are going to build a skyscraper, the easy part - the fun part - is imagining what the momentous building will look like. But before you start dreaming about fluorescent corridors and towering steel rods, the first thing you do is plan your foundation, plumbing and electrical circuits. It is only after thoughtful planning that you actually begin pouring concrete and pounding nails.

Sales is the same. You must build systematically. However appealing it might be to leap forward and start throwing sales pitches left and right. Random acts of selling don't work. You can't just jump in and start swinging the diamond presentation hammer improvising as you go. You must plan and build on a solid strategic foundation then you can worry about execution.

I respect your time and truly appreciate that you are investing some of your busy life into reading what I have to say. Every page and every story have a purpose. I urge you to stay focused as you move through this book or you may miss some key insights.

Once you enter the world of Adornment you will find that the way you think about jewelry sales will be changed forever. I would say to enjoy the journey, but we already know you will don't we?

CHAPTER 2: PMA

Your work is going to fill a large part of your life, and the only way to be truly satisfied is to do what you believe is great work. And the only way to do great work is to love what you do.
Steve Jobs

You and I both know that there is something special about diamond sales. It isn't easy, but the results are always worth it. You are reading this because you are a little bit more dedicated to your own personal growth than your peers.

Isn't it true?

Aren't you HUNGRY right now to grow, to earn more, to reach the next level and have more confidence in yourself? Lots of people SAY they are.

But most people are just onlookers, right?

You take action which is why you are always trying to LEARN and get the edge. You invest in yourself. You are decisive and committed. Long ago you decided personal and professional development was HUGELY

IMPORTANT at this stage in your life. You DEEPLY care about reaching a new level of success. You are the type of person, I'm guessing, who really wants to learn more, love more, give more, make your mark. You are a lot like Yogi Berra.

Yogi Berra was an 18-time Baseball All-Star and won 10 World Series championships as a player—more than any other player in MLB history. When asked what made him so successful, he said, "90% of baseball is mental. The other half is physical." While this formula may not make sense mathematically the fundamentals associated with it applies whether it is baseball, relationships, sales or any other aspect of your life. The principles that are driving this formula are always relevant.

Of course, there is a physical side to sales. Product knowledge, presentation skills, showing tools- these are all vital for achieving sales success. But in the end, the biggest factor of your own success is your mental game. You, and only you, have the complete ability to control your attitude. The fact of the matter is that selling is a tough business. The economy is always bouncing up and down. Your competition is after your customers and they are tough to beat. Sales professionals hear no's every single day and for many it can feel devastating after so many of these are stacked one upon the other. With these forces at play, it isn't uncommon for sales professionals to feel inadequate, to lose their aspirations and even come to the point where they doubt their own abilities.

All of us are going to have these kinds of self-doubt and setbacks. That's right, even Susan who smiles constantly and has sunshine as an attitude is going to feel like they can't do it from time to time. When this happens, go dust-off the old VCR you have laying around in your grandma's house and pop in Sylvester Stallone's 1974 movie, Rocky. Watch as he gets battered and beaten unceasingly. Lean in and listen to the man who knows what it is like to feel to stare defeat in the face.

"Let me tell you something you already know. The world ain't all sunshine and rainbows. It's a very mean and nasty place and I don't care how tough you are it will beat you to your knees and keep you there permanently if you let it.

"You, me, or nobody is gonna hit as hard as life. But it ain't about how hard ya hit. It's about how hard you can get hit and keep moving forward. How much you can take and keep moving forward. That's how winning is done!

"You don't allow life's hits to define who you are. This is what makes you successful, you recognize that you control your reactions. You control how you feel when something doesn't go this way.

"Now if you know what you're worth then go out and get what you're worth. But ya gotta be willing to take the hits, and not pointing fingers saying you ain't where you wanna be because of him, or her, or anybody! Cowards do that and that ain't you! You're better than that!"

All of us are going to feel human emotions that tell us we are not good enough or that today is going to be a bad day, but like Rocky said, what is going to separate the champions from the rest of the herd is going to be your mental and emotional discipline. This is fantastic news because a positive mental attitude (PMA) is entirely in your control!

Being positive about your situation is going to keep you focused and constructive to your team, even when all seems bleak. You will build up those around you and you are going to reap the benefits of your belief that today is a good day.

To begin building your foundation of developing a positive mental attitude there are four essential cornerstones for you to achieve your ultimate mental and emotional strength.

1. Believe in your product.

When you are passionate about the products and services that you are offering and are unabashedly enthusiastic about the value and benefit they bring to your customers it will be easy to sell. Yes, it is important to study closing techniques, features and benefits, and driving profit for your company, but what is more important is to let your customers know that what you have to bring to the table is exceptional in every sense of the word. Your passion is going to be contagious. Customers will come crawling to you because of that desire to help and improve their lives. You have the good news. The news that diamonds are valuable and that they are going to say what your love cannot articulate by only using words.

2. Believe in your training

What you are learning right here and right now by reading this book is making you a better salesman. What you do and say every time you interact with a customer is teaching you how you can improve. Effective training and learning is key to success. Those who become satisfied with the status quo and do things because that is how they have always done them will soon be left behind and find themselves penniless with their heads spinning wondering where they went wrong.

Blockbuster was offered to buy Netflix for $51 million in its early stages. Blockbuster turned down the offer. They liked what they were doing and didn't see the need to change. Fast forward twenty years and Netflix is currently valued at over $151 billion while Blockbuster closed its doors forever. It's only fitting that whether it was a PR stunt or not, the final film rented from Blockbuster on Nov 9, 2013 was "This Is the End". If a multimillion-dollar corporation can sink to its knees because of enjoying the status quo than so will you if you get too comfortable.

Anyone can read through a book, check out a spreadsheet or watch a presentation and come away with a general grasp of product knowledge and sales techniques. What makes champions are those that dive in headfirst and apply what it is that they learn. They take notes. They watch other sales presentations and notice what it is they like and dislike about different sales pitches. They ask for help and have others watch them present to find constructive ways to improve.

When you do this, your confidence in yourself is going to hit the stars.

3. Believe in your company

Whether you work in a ma and pa shop in the middle of nowhere or you are part of an international entity you need to believe in it. Culture and atmosphere are something that can build or destroy sales teams. You need to have a strong commitment as a team to outstanding customer service to your customers and an even stronger commitment to your team. The joy of selling quickly evaporates when customers feel like they are talking to snake charmers or there is infighting because of office politics.

Sharks are not permitted. Period. Stealing other's sales or splitting sales that you made minimum impact on are poison. Be empowering. Be encouraging. Be the coworker you wish you had. Then watch as you make the first step to becoming a better cohort that your teammates begin improving as well. Together, you will make more sales.

Together, you will make more money.

The final cornerstone is the most integral to the structure of your attitude towards yourself.

4. Believe in yourself

There are entire books dedicated to having you believe in yourself, and I am not going to pretend that I have the one secret ingredient that is going to boost you to new levels of self-love. However, believing in yourself is the holy grail of creating and maintaining a consistently positive mental focus. It is the foundation of your entire sales career. Without it, everything can crumble down around you.

No matter the situation you find yourself in, you are going to be in control. The situations will not dictate how you act or respond, it is what you believe about the situation that will cause you to react to it. When you have a positive mental attitude then having that optimistic outlook in every situation is going to attract positive changes and increase your levels of achievement.

Nobody is more qualified than you. Don't listen to the critics.

Brene Brown has a special on Netflix entitled "The Call to Courage" (if you have an hour of free time, I highly recommend that you watch it) where she gives a quote from Theodore Roosevelt, the 26th President of the United States of America. This is what he has to say about listening to the critics,

"It is not the critic who counts; not the man who points out how the strong man stumbles, or where the doer of deeds could have done them better. The credit belongs to the man who is actually in the arena, whose face is marred by dust and sweat and blood; who strives valiantly; who errs, who comes short again and again, because there is no effort without error and shortcoming; but who does actually strive to do the deeds; who knows great enthusiasms, the great devotions; who spends himself in a worthy cause; who at the best knows in the end the triumph of high achievement, and who at the worst, if he fails, at least fails while daring greatly, so that his place shall never be with those cold and timid souls who neither know victory nor defeat."

Criticism is cheap. Your mother, cousins, friends, Twitter Tim, anybody can criticize. In today's world there are millions of people in the cheap seats saying that you aren't good enough and that you aren't doing it right. Pay them no mind. They are not out in the arena discovering what techniques work, what sells and what doesn't. Criticism is easy. Creating something of value is significantly more difficult. It's easy for the fat viewers on the couch to find a flaw in a professional football players footwork, but overall, isn't that player the more impressive one? We can easily hear when a singer hits a wrong note, but if we're tone deaf ourselves, why insult somebody who has worked so hard to sing as well as they do?

What you do each and every day is worthwhile, and you are good at it. We place far too much emphasis on other people's opinions about us, often to the exclusion of our own. This takes away from our own personal power. No matter what anybody says about you, it doesn't hold any significance to who you truly are unless you identify or agree with them. So, stop identifying with other people's opinions and become aware of how you see yourself. Nobody knows you better than you do. Never accept another person's reality as your own. Always believe that you can achieve anything you put your mind to. And, most importantly, never let another person's opinion of you affect what you believe about yourself.

Even with this in mind, remember that there is such a thing as constructive criticism. Listen to those who are trying to help you reach your full potential AND who know what they are talking about. Nobody has the perfect sales pitch, but maybe your boss has an insight into how you could improve your use of the counter pad. Listen for understanding. Gain as much benefit as you can from it.

Speaking of listening, listen to what I must tell you.
You CAN sell.
You ARE improving.
You are the MASTER of your destiny.

By the time you finish this book you are going to know that you are more than enough. If you must compare yourself to someone else, let it be a person who is less fortunate, and let it be a lesson to learn just how abundant your life truly is. It's just a matter of perspective. You may find that you are not entirely grateful for what you possess. You may believe that you need more than you have right now to be happy. If this is the case, then you are absolutely right—you will need more, and you will continue to need more.

This cycle will perpetuate if your mind believes it to be true. If you focus on what you have, and not on what you lack, you will always have enough, because you will always be enough. You can stay at one place in your life, never learning new skills and going around and around in one place repeating the same mistakes, 'stuck' in a rut. Or you learn new skills and then move forwards and upwards in your life.

When your feet hit the floor in the morning you are going to tell yourself that today is going to be a good day.

You are going to rock it. You are going to have a good day in the store. You are going to show just the right piece to just the right person. That person is going to buy. You are going to make a sale today. You are going to make a customer for life. You are going to be the best salesman in your company. You are going to be successful. You are going to recognize your worth. Rocky said,

"Now if you know what you're worth then go out and get what you're worth. But ya gotta be willing to take the hits, and not pointing fingers saying you ain't where you wanna be because of him, or her, or anybody! Cowards do that and that ain't you! You're better than that!"

It is not going to be easy. You are going to have to leave sticky notes in your mirror to remind yourself to be positive. You are going to see the storm clouds come and have to really search to find that silver lining. Each day is going to present us with new and different challenges. But that is what makes life so fun to live, because we get to overcome what we couldn't yesterday.

Each of us are different and we are going to have to find our own ways to maintain that positive mental attitude. If you believe in your product, your training, your company and most importantly if you can believe in yourself, you are going to find that you are amazing at selling jewelry. Folks are drawn to the people who are more upbeat and are excited by what they do. That is going to be you. You got this. I believe in you, do you?

CHAPTER 3: DIAMONDS

Live as if you were to die tomorrow. Learn as if you were to live forever.
Mahatma Gandhi

Now that you are ready to commit to becoming a more professional jeweler the best place to start your transformation is by understanding what it is you sell. Now I know what you are thinking, "But I already know everything that there is to know about diamonds". If you had this same thought than I applaud your advanced knowledge. However, knowing is not enough.

You have to love it.

I want you to look at diamonds the way that college juniors look at a freshly made pizza with that lustful glint in their eyes. Sales is always better when you sell something that you believe in. It is not scary. Selling something you don't believe in is Freddy Kruger scary.

When you're selling something that you don't have faith in everything will be more difficult. It will be harder to close, harder to show and harder to make a living selling diamonds if you don't believe in them. So how do you earn that faith back? You need to treat diamonds like you are on your first date with them. Learn as much as you can about them.

Diamonds, precious gems and gold are so fascinating that you could be reading a book dedicated entirely to just how it is that they came to be. They have such a rich history and have impacted the lives of your ancestors since we first came wandering out of our caves looking for food. Anyone can have their five minutes of fame, but these guys have always been in the spotlight.

So, start thinking about building your relationship. Take diamonds out on that first date again. Study their intricate, mathematically calculated curves. Stare deep into their soul and be mesmerized by the way you are drawn into its soul.

Once you become close enough you are going to fall in love. It is going to be contagious. Your customers will be just as head over heels for it as you are, and you are going to sell a lot of diamonds. So, sit down and dive deep into the mysterious world of the diamond.

The Industry

No other industry has the emotional, historical or interconnected product ties to the human race than the luxury jewelry industry. In this world there are two main categories of interest: diamonds and colored gemstones. Diamonds are at the forefront of one's mind when they wish to express their love to another. So diamonds are where we will start our journey. They are cultivating, mesmerizing and going to make you a truck load of money.

Unlike most gifts, the materials for jewelry are born

deep within the Earth and then artfully displayed so that we can admire a piece's beauty for generations. You are more than just a salesman offering a product that is opened and enjoyed for just the one day. You are offering to be a part of a memory that is at the heart of a couple's love story. This makes everything you sell unique, timeless and something that is meant to be passed down from generation to generation.

Unfortunately, your customers do not know that.

Most shoppers walk into a store and assume that all jewelry pieces, especially diamonds, are roughly the same. Like a slightly different iPhone that has just come off the assembly line. They could not be more wrong. Diamonds are not simply put into a mold and sent down the assembly line or picked off a tree like apples. They are born-much like you and I - with unique birthmarks and personalities shaped by a lifetime of adventure. So, when someone asks you about the value and quality of a diamond each answer you give will be unique depending on the particular diamond piece you are showing. This makes diamond presentations much more personal and intimate than any other purchase a customer will make in their lifetime.

Learning more about diamonds will make you more confident, more interesting and more effective when selling diamonds. It may even surprise you how much more you will learn to appreciate and value what you get to sell every day.

Tale as Old as Time
Diamonds could also be the oldest thing that one can buy. The youngest diamonds found to date are roughly one billion years old and the oldest ones are about 3.3 billion years old. Once you consider that the Earth has been estimated to be over 4.5 billion years old, you realize

that they have seen some stuff (i.e. what killed the dinosaurs, the infamous ice age and the rise of your favorite celebrity).

Not only are they old, they are tough. Perhaps you have seen on Pinterest or Instagram the caption, "A diamond is just a piece of coal that did well under pressure." Inspiring isn't it? Well, as inspiring as it might be, a diamond would not appreciate it when you compare its struggle to your high school breakup. The pressure that diamonds experienced were between 650,000 and 870,000 psi (pounds per square inch). We could compare this to the pressure that the Seattle Seahawks defense put on Payton Manning during Super Bowl XLVIII or that the average pressure on the floor of the Pacific Ocean is only about 5,500 psi. It would also be good to note that no human has ever been to the deepest part of the Pacific Ocean.

On top of this pressure that would make the pressure your parents put on you to live up to their expectations look insignificant, they also must deal with tremendous amounts of heat. Diamonds cannot form their intricate crystalline structures without being bombarded with temperatures ranging from 1,700 to 2,400 degrees Fahrenheit.

Conditions of this extreme are not found anywhere you and I will ever walk. This region that achieves the necessary pressure and the optimal temperature for diamond crystallization is known as the diamond stability field that is located roughly 90 to 120 miles below your feet.

In the diamond stability field, scientists have a good idea of how the diamonds are born, but it is all based on recent discoveries. What we do know, is that not all diamonds are created equal. Each grew at its own rate and in its own time. In a laboratory setting, one-carat lab-grown diamonds are created in a day or two with some laboratories taking a little less than three weeks. In nature, we can estimate the amount of time it took a diamond to fully develop by studying its grain pattern. With this knowledge we have discovered that some diamonds in nature also formed in less than a day while some of the more high-quality gems are estimated to have taken centuries to fully develop.

Most Are Rejects

While tumbling in the massive, violent forces in the planet's interior there are a million things that could have gone wrong. It's a miracle that diamonds exist at all. Most diamonds were swallowed up and pulverized before we ever had the chance of discovering them. Of those that survived, only about a fraction are gem quality. The majority of mined diamonds are so small, so impure or didn't crystallize properly that they are unrecognizable as diamonds. The only use we have for them is for industrial purposes such as diamond drill bits and other abrasives.

On occasion, you may have an interested customer who may wonder how diamonds got from this big diamond incubator, called the diamond stability field, that lies deep beneath the ancient cores of our continent and came up here to the point where they are minable?

The answer. Depends.

Some diamonds decided that they were tired of living with other diamonds and were carried upward to the surface via lava tubes. In those cases, most of the diamonds turned into graphite or burned up entirely. For a lucky few, the magma's special chemistry prevented this from happening. In those situations, the magma contained high amounts of pressurized gases and liquids such as carbon dioxide and water. As the magma moved upward toward the surface, these expanded, "refrigerating" the diamonds and saving them from destruction.

These lava tubes are a primary location for diamond hunters to discover their sparkling treasure. With time, these lava tubes will eventually succumb to erosion and be carried down rivers to what we call secondary sites. Secondary sites usually have much higher quality diamonds because those who were flawed did not survive being carried away from the primary sites. That is why many large diamond operations are found on beaches and the mouths of large rivers.

There's another aspect of this topic that you may want to highlight, too. Diamonds have always come from places at the frontiers of human imagination. In ancient times, they embodied the fabulous wealth of the Far East. Today they beckon from frozen Arctic wilderness where Russia leads the world in diamonds contributing more than 20 % of the world's output per carat weight. They hail from sun-scorched deserts of South Africa, and ocean depths near Botswana. Even the closest mines that can be found in Canada are well above the Arctic circle. This kind of information can add "faraway places" to other elements of a diamond's romantic appeal.

Because of their exotic appeal mined diamonds have sometimes been used to fuel conflict and war. The Kimberley Process Certification Scheme protects the world from these conflict diamonds. Although there are very few diamonds that could ever be considered conflict diamonds the media has portrayed them as a huge deal to the diamond community. Millennials are especially keen to know that no wars, child slavery or murder were used to get your diamonds into your store. The chance of a conflict diamond reaching your store is almost zero. You are ethically sourced, environmentally cautious, and knowledgeable about all your diamonds and their sources.

While diamonds are forever-- their natural reserves aren't. Over the next decade or so, several the diamond deposits now being mined will be completely depleted. Although mining methods are increasing in efficiency, prospects for new deposits and mines are uncertain. As a result, world diamond production may hold steady, or perhaps decline. Sometime in the next few years Argyle Diamonds, Australia's biggest diamond mine and the source of rare and prized fancy pink gems, will come to the end of its life. With its death goes 10% of all annual diamond output. Diamonds don't just spring from the ground. They are rare and exotic.

Customers might be interested to hear that through studying diamonds geologists have made fascinating discoveries about the earth, its formation, and its history. All these wonderful advances in human knowledge came from diamond inclusions. Inclusions are any part of the diamond that has not been properly crystalized or other elements that have been absorbed into the diamonds as they formed. These inclusions act as a time capsule to the past and have allowed scientists to look into the earth and see the changes in pressure, temperature and temperament. Speaking of science, we are going to delve more into why diamonds are so freaking cool.

Scientifically Fascinating
In laboratory tests we have discovered that your typical gem-quality diamonds are around 99.95% pure carbon with some being up to 99.99% pure. This makes diamonds one of the purest of all materials found in nature. Diamond is the only gem that is composed of entirely one element. All other gems are chemical combinations of multiple elements. For example, corundum -ruby and

sapphire- are made primarily of aluminum and oxygen with a chemical formula of Al_2O_3. Other gems, such as tourmaline, are far more complex with the chemical formula equivalent of a calculus math problem:
$(Na,Ca)(Mg,Li,Al,Fe2+)3(Al,Mg,Cr)6(BO3)3Si6O18(OH)4$

Not only is its purity incredibly rare to find in nature, its anatomical structure makes it perfectly symmetrical in every direction. This special structure makes it different than the graphite in your pencil even though they are both made of pure carbon.

In a diamond, the carbon atoms are arranged tetrahedrally. Each carbon atom is attached to four other carbon atoms 1.544 x 10-10 meter away with a C-C-C bond angle of 109.5 degrees. It is a strong, rigid three-dimensional structure that results in an infinite network of atoms. This accounts for diamond's hardness, extraordinary strength and durability and gives diamond a higher density than graphite (3.514 grams per cubic centimeter).

Because of its tetrahedral structure, diamond also shows a great resistance to compression. The hardness of a crystal is measured on a scale, devised by Friedrich Mohs, which ranks compounds according to their ability to scratch one another. Diamond will scratch all other materials and is the hardest material known (designated as 10 on the Mohs scale).

Diamonds are also the best conductor of heat that we know, conducting up to five times the amount that copper does. It also conducts sound, but not electricity; it is an insulator, and its electrical resistance, optical transmissivity and chemical inertness are correspondingly remarkable.

When you compare the carbon atoms in graphite you

will find that the atoms of graphite are also arranged in an infinite array. However, instead of a tetrahedral design, graphite is layered. These planar arrangements extend in two dimensions to form a horizontal, hexagonal "chicken-wire" array. These layered arrays are held together by weaker forces. Combining the layered chicken wire structure with weak bonds allows graphite electrons to move easily within the planes. This permits graphite to conduct electricity and heat as well as absorb light and, unlike diamond, appear black in color.

This three-dimensional structure also accounts for the physical properties of graphite. So unlike diamond, graphite can be used as a lubricant or in pencils because the weak layers cleave readily. It is soft and slippery, and its hardness is less than a one on the Mohs scale. Graphite also has a lower density (2.266 grams per cubic centimeter) than diamond.

There you have a fun breakdown of how diamond is so radically different from graphite even though they are made of the same substance. Diamond is stronger, tougher, and rarer because of its special tetrahedral structure. Along with being strong, this tetrahedral structure in diamonds is also what makes it so stunning because it has the special ability to slow down light. When light passes the diamond, it slows down by 40% and once it exits the diamond it bursts back to its original speed. Combine this with a diamonds unique refractive index and the gemstone acts like a prism to separate white light into an explosion of colorful rainbow. All of this accounts for the unique "fire" of a diamond and is unrivaled in its brilliance and scintillation.

Do not fall prey to ads that claim diamond simulants, such as cubic zirconia and moissanite, surpassing diamonds in their scintillation! The basis of this claim boils down to dispersion rates. A diamond's dispersion is measured to be 0.044 and these diamond simulants have a higher dispersion rate.

Advertisers are trying to steer the public eye away from diamonds and towards these less remarkable substitutes because of this one solitary "improvement". What these simulants will never be able to surpass is a diamonds direct connection to love and commitment. Is your love as pure and long lasting as a diamond or is it fake? Not something I would ask a customer, but recognize your emotions when you ask yourself that question. Diamonds are deeply tied to our relationships.

THE 4 C's

As you have most likely already learned, there are four C's that go into grading diamonds. The grades that these diamonds receive tell us how rare and unique they are. This section is going to give you the information necessary to better understand the grading system. Once you understand this your ability to build value in diamonds is going to skyrocket. The reason for this is because a G colored VSI one carat RB is as gibberish to shoppers as me speaking Russian to you would be. When you take the time to explain each part of the 4 C's you effectively:

• Minimize confusion and uncertainty.
• Create greater value and appreciation for diamonds.
• Guide your customer to wanting to make a purchase.
• Build confidence in the customer's perception of your professionalism

Carat
Carat is most easily understood as how much the diamond weighs. Having a one carat diamond means that the diamond weighs one carat. Carats are an extremely accurate measurement. One carat equals 7/1000 ounce, or

if you are more familiar with the metric system 0.200 (⅕) gram. This is incredibly light. To put it in perspective, a single jellybean weighs 1.1 grams which means a jellybean is 5.5 times heavier than a one carat diamond!

Each carat is then divided into 100 equal portions called points. Think of these points as being like pennies in a dollar. One penny/point is 0.01 carats or 1/100 carat. Fifty pennies/points are 0.5 carats or ½ carat. One hundred pennies are 1 carat. 120 pennies/points are 1.2 carats and so on and so forth. Companies can use either a decimal or fraction system to show the weight in carats as company policy will vary. Decide amongst your sales team which system is best for you and your customers.

Diamonds are weighed using these precise measurements because a fraction of a difference in weight can be the difference of hundreds - sometimes thousands - of dollars in value.

When comparing two diamonds, please note that just because one is twice the carat weight of the other does not mean that it will appear to be twice the size. It is only twice the amount of weight. It works the exact same regarding cost. Going from a one-carat diamond to a two-carat diamond doesn't mean that the price will be double. In fact, going from a one-carat diamond to a two-carat diamond can sometimes be 7x the difference in dollar amounts.

The reason for this big difference in cost is rarity. The chances of finding a diamond are 1 in 10,000,000. The chances of finding a diamond that is roughly one carat are 1 in 1,000,000,000. That is one chance in a billion. With odds like that it is a miracle that even average Joe has the option of investing in such a treasure!

The carat system of measuring is quite ancient. Carat comes from the word carob. Carobs are trees that man has cultivated in the Mediterranean area for over 4,000 years. The carob seeds themselves are inedible, but traders noticed that the seeds were naturally uniform in both size and weight. The seeds were used to balance scales when traders weighed precious gemstones, where the tiniest change in weight made a noticeable difference. A higher number of seeds indicated a heavier and therefore more valuable stone.

Granted, we no longer weigh diamonds with such archaic mechanisms, but this tradition has held true to the present day. In 1907 it was agreed upon and adapted universally for gemstones to be weighed in carats.

Sometimes you may hear the word melee be used in casual conversation in the diamond world. A melee is a cut diamond that weighs less than ⅕ carat or 20 points. These melee diamonds can be accent diamonds on the band of an engagement ring, in a drawer of similar size for quick repair purposes, or a part of a young diamond enthusiast's collection. Don't throw this word around willy-nilly but knowing it can make you sound competent in conversation with fellow jewelers. Any other jewelry jargon will be learned as you progress, grow and find a use for them in your day to day life.

Color
With an effective explanation of color, you can highlight the natural wonder of your product, demonstrate your knowledge and skill, illuminate one of the mysteries of value, and help your customer take a step toward a satisfying purchase decision.

Much like you and I, diamonds are born to be unique and have their own shades of color. For diamonds, a large part of their value comes from their unique shades and saturation. Diamonds can come in all shades of the rainbow. The most common types of diamonds are yellow and brown throughout and are quite abundant in nature. The rarest color is a deep, ruby like red. There have only been around thirty red colored diamonds ever discovered!

In your jewelry store you will mostly be working with diamonds ranging from yellow to completely colorless. Just about every diamond has a faint tint of color in them. Completely colorless diamonds are quite rare. This is because colorless diamonds have to be born in conditions as ideal as possible. Under no other circumstances will you find a colorless diamond.

This does not mean that colorful diamonds are of any less importance or value. Some of the most sought-after colors in the world are currently deep yellows, pinks, and blues. Collectors are always on the lookout for something unique, so it is a good idea to have some pigment options in your case.

Much like with carats, small hue differences cause spikes in price. The GIA grades diamonds on a scale of D (colorless) through Z (fairly yellow in color). If you don't have a GIA color grading chart get one immediately.

Colorless: Grades D, E, and F
D, E and F graded diamonds are of the creme de la creme of the clear diamond colors. Sometimes referred to as completely "white" diamonds these grades command the highest price due to their rarity. While there are differences in color between D, E, and F diamonds, those minute differences usually only be detected by a trained gemologist in side by side comparisons, and rarely by the untrained eye.

D-F diamonds are going to show just how fabulous and rare they are when they are set in white gold / platinum. When a D-F diamond is set in Rose gold or yellow gold there is going to be a slight reflection of color from the gold up into the diamond which will negate the diamond's colorless effect.

Once you know this you can show the colorless grades true potential. Be sure that when you show mounted D-F diamonds that you are showing them ones that are set in white gold or platinum. When you show loose colorless diamonds be sure that they have set the perfect stage with a diamond on the lower end of the spectrum so that they can have something to immediately compare with. Without something to compare it to it is difficult to see just how different, better and special these diamonds truly are.

Near Colorless: G, H, I and J

These diamonds contain slightly higher concentrations of nitrogen which will show a slight "warmth" to them. To most people these are nearly indistinguishable from the D-F grade. Because of this, these are very easy to sell when you point out that you can cut a lot of cost out of a diamond going from colorless to a near colorless. These are more common to find in nature with I and J grade diamonds often retailing for half the price of a D colored diamond. Each jump down from G decreases the price anywhere from 10-20%.

Faint Color: K, L and M

K diamonds are typically when diamonds show a lot more warmth that is more recognizable to the average Joe, color (usually a yellow tint). This is not necessarily a bad thing. Many of your customers are going to find it very appealing. To some, diamonds that are warmer will feel more real and natural. Perfectly colorless diamonds to some are going to remind them of almost fake jewelry. By assumption most of your customers are not used to living in a world of colorless diamonds.

Once again, we also see a jump in price with these being more common to find in nature. K diamonds are often half the price of a G colored diamond.

Very Light Color: N O P Q and R
Diamonds in the N-R color range have an easily seen yellow or brown tint but are much less expensive than higher grades.

Light Color: S T U V W X Y Z
Diamonds in the S-Z color range are the easiest to see their yellow or brown saturation. Any darker and these diamonds would be on their own canary yellow and chocolate brown color grading scales. These are often the least sold of your diamonds because of their low demand and abundance.

Some of your customers will be curious as to why the grading scale does not go from A-Z and instead goes from D-Z. This is because before the GIA color grading scale we have today there were several different grading scales used throughout the world. Different scales graded diamonds differently with some being AAA, AA, A, B, and C or 0, 1, 2, 3, 4 and it created a lot of confusion. GIA stepped in and proposed their grading scale that would throw out the confusion and not use any of the past grading types that used AAA, AA, A, B and C.

There is also a physiological advantage to starting the grading system with the letter D. The letter A is associated in our minds with the very best, the cream of the crop. By default, anything beneath an A grade would seem subpar. Even showing someone a B diamond can give the impression that there is an A diamond out there and feel that their B grade diamond is inferior in some unknown way. Starting at D erases any preconceived notions such as these and allows you to better show color.

Tips and Tricks of Selling Color.

Before jumping into color, it is always appropriate to ask your customer if they are familiar with how a diamond is graded. Most likely they will respond by saying that they have done some research, but they aren't entirely confident in how it is important. You should be excited because you are about to take them to jewel school.

First, compliment them taking the time to research.

"Not a lot of people take the time to research diamonds before they come in. You should be proud to be one of the smart ones. Let me help you understand it a little better now that we can see actual diamonds in front of us."

Next to you should be an easily read chart that shows the GIA color grading scale. When you show your customer how to read it start by placing your finger on the Z and then slide it up to the D. This shows your customer two things:

- As you go up the alphabet you are getting something better
- 'D' is where you want to be because that is where you finished.

This happens because in your customer's mind they are going to liken it to a race. You start at the starting line which is Z and you want to go as far as you can to finish at D. The finish line is where all the celebrating happens and where the party is. Nobody wants to quit the race halfway through. They are going to want to finish it right?

From there have two different diamonds with a clear and obvious distinction between the two. Don't show two diamonds that are close in color because then you will make them feel like an idiot when they can't tell an immediate difference. They will lose confidence in you and even worse you will kill their confidence in themselves. Once that is gone it is difficult to rebuild that self-confidence needed for your customer to follow you through all the way through the sale.

There are several things you need to keep in mind when showing color. The first thing you need to remember is that color becomes much harder to detect once a stone is set in a ring and placed in an environment that contains color. For instance, an H color diamond may look as colorless as a D when set in a ring under normal lighting conditions, even though they are five points different on the GIA color scale. Especially if the two are not compared side by side.

Yellow gold makes slight amounts of yellow in a diamond less obvious, while white metal mountings make yellow diamonds more apparent.

Color becomes more important as carat weight increases, because color is easier to perceive in a larger diamond, and lower color grade diamonds make great price points for someone who has a lower budget and doesn't mind color.

Clarity
This is where most purchasers have a difficult time wrapping their head around diamonds and their prices. Clarity in its most basic definition is the measure of imperfections in the crystal structure and mineral impurities trapped inside the stone.

Diamonds are made underground, so if you think about it, the fact that there are diamonds out there that are completely clean is mind-blowing.

For the best value, select a diamond with inclusions that can't be seen through the crown without magnification (also known as eye-clean diamonds), such as a SI or VS clarity grade. These diamonds are much less expensive than the extremely rare Flawless (FL) or Internally Flawless (IF) diamonds.

Diamond Shape — Some diamond shapes require a higher clarity grade than others. Emerald and Ascher-shaped diamonds (referred to as step cut) are designed with rectangular facets that emphasize transparency and let you see farther down into the diamond, which can make inclusions more visible. For these diamond shapes, choose a clarity grade of VS1 or better to ensure inclusions will not be visible.

Conversely, round, princess, oval, marquise, pear, and heart-shaped diamonds may not require as high of a clarity grade. Cut with a brilliant facet pattern, which reflects light from many different angles, these shapes naturally hide many inclusions.

Diamond Size — As diamond size increases, the size of the facets (the multiple mirror-like surfaces on the diamond) also increases. This can make inclusions more visible. Be sure to prioritize a higher clarity grade as the size of your diamond increases.

Cut
The Most Important Investment for a Diamond
The investment made in cutting a diamond is arguably the most important and it's certainly the key that unlocks a diamond's potential beauty. When they come from the

mine, most diamonds look like frosted pebbles – or even pieces of broken bottle glass. By the time they leave the cutter's wheel, they're radiant gemstones cut with mathematical precision to best reflect even the weakest of star's glow.

The cutting process represents centuries of technical evolution. No one knows who originally discovered the art of diamond cutting. Humans employed similar techniques to shape hard materials back in the Stone Age. What we do know is that primitive diamond fashioning have occurred in India for thousands of years. More modern diamond cutting began to evolve in Italy during the 1300s. By the year 1700 most of the basic concepts and methods had been developed. Except for the speed and precision made possible by technological advances, many of those methods have changed little since then. Even high-tech operations follow essentially the same steps that all cutters have followed for the past five centuries.

If you tell customers that diamond is the hardest material on Earth, some might ask, "Then how can they be cut at all?" Simply put, diamonds are cut using other diamonds.

Cutting diamonds isn't done by rubbing two diamonds together and seeing what happens to the other. Instead, diamonds are ground up into crystal fragments called diamond dust or diamond grit. To polish a diamond, the cutter masterfully orients it so soft crystal directions are exposed. The millions of grit particles on the polishing wheel are randomly oriented. The laws of probability guarantee that many of the particles will have hard directions turned toward the diamond being polished. By pressing the two together you cut diamond through what's essentially microscopic scratching.

Diamond cutters are not only required to be skilled technical artists, but they're also smart businesspeople. One of their prime objectives is to produce maximum value from every rough diamond they handle. That means transforming the natural features of the crystal into the best combination of 4Cs in the finished gemstone.

Cutters will eliminate inclusions or position them for minimum visibility, but they have to work with the diamond that they are given. Even proportions can be varied slightly to increase weight yield, but significant variations will hurt the diamond's visual appeal. Every cut is deliberate, planned out weeks in advance, and done with a meticulous hand.

Diamonds of exceptional size and quality warrant careful examination and thoughtful creativity. Planning may take days – perhaps weeks – to complete. The cutter might polish an initial facet, called a window. This allows the diamond's interior to be examined for major inclusions, and also for clues that indicate the grain. For diamonds likely to go down in the history books, practice models are sometimes made from glass or other simulant materials such as CZ so that every micro-scratch is planned in advance.

Much like a master chess player picking the best of a thousand possible moves, the cutter examines the crystal, evaluates the variables, and decides what needs to be done.

From the time it takes a diamond to be cut, sanded, and polished it will lose 40% of its original weight. I.e. a 1.00 carat diamond cut will be a 0.60 carat diamond on display.

One of the very first cuts made to a diamond is by cutting it in half. A large number of diamond crystals are divided at least once. There are two ways to divide a diamond:

• Cleaving – Using force to split the diamond in a weak crystal direction.
• Sawing – Using a metal blade and diamond grit, or intense heat from a laser, to cut through the crystal.

Cleaving is as brutal and even more complex than you imagine. It is so much more than simply hacking away at a miniscule diamond with an ax. It involves a careful examination, thought out strategy, and careful concussive force. Because of the internal structure of diamonds, they have areas in them where they can be broken along a plane. Experts discover the internal grain of the diamond, find those cleavage points and simply hit those points to split diamonds cleanly along those planes.

Sawing is not quite as risky as cleaving. A blade that is used to cut a diamond in half is 4-6 inches in diameter, but less than 1/100-inch-thick (that is just slightly thicker than a piece of paper which is 4/1000 inch thick). It turns at speeds of about 3,000 to 8,000 RPMs. At those speeds a one-carat crystal typically takes from 4–6 hours to saw through. Sometimes, however, the blade encounters a knot (another diamond crystal included in the larger crystal) or the grain reverses in a twinned crystal. When this happens, it may be necessary to remove the diamond, remount it in, and then saw from another direction.

Lasers are becoming more and more common as the technology has improved. Lasers can cut the sewing time in half and eliminated the issues caused by grain reverses or knots. They can also produce novelty shapes such as flowers, paw prints and other unique shapes. However, cutting a 1 carat diamond in half still takes 2-3 hours per diamond. These guys are tough.

Once the basic shape is done, the rest becomes more of an artistic expression than an actual science. I am not going to go into any more depth when it comes to the craftsmanship of diamonds because there is so much that goes into it and I want to give you information that is immediately helpful to improve your diamond sales. However, if you would like to read up more on the polishing and shaping process you can read up on them by giving it a google search. Trust me, it's fascinating.

When all is said and done 60% of a diamonds value is in its cut. No surprise there.

When thinking of diamonds, many will immediately think of the classic round diamond shape. It's no doubt that the round brilliant cut is the most popular shape. However, it isn't the only shape of diamond on the market. If you're looking for something different, there are plenty of other shapes available. A diamond's shape refers to its physical form and each diamond shape is very different, possessing unique characteristics.

Round Brilliant
The round brilliant cut diamond is the most popular shape of diamond, accounting for more than half of all diamonds sold today. The round brilliant is the most researched cut in the industry. It is the culmination of thousands of years of art and mathematical precision. Diamond cutters have used advanced scientific theories of light reflection and precise mathematical calculations to optimize its fire and brilliance. The round brilliant is the most versatile of all cuts both in terms of style and value. With more fire and brilliance than any other shape, this cut offers the ideal balance between cut, color and clarity grades and budget. For a bachelor unsure of what might please his lady, it is hard to go wrong with this classic

choice.

Princess Cut

Princess cut diamonds are exceptionally brilliant because of the way they are cut and are available in both square and rectangular shapes. The color that is emitted from princess cut diamonds is unique. While the color of other diamond is displayed mainly in the center, the princess cut diamonds show distinct color in each of the corners as well. Because of its extra facets, the Princess cut can disperse more light through the stone, this serves to hide inclusions more efficiently, making it the most brilliant of all square- and rectangular-shaped stones.

In regard to diamond clarity, both the princess cut diamond and the round brilliant diamonds are similar in that they hide inclusions decently. It is imperative to know that princess cut diamonds have serious issues with durability, as its four sharp corners chip easier. An inclusion in any of the four corners increases that risk for chipping.

Oval Cut

Oval cut diamonds have a classic appearance with a modern twist! It is a popular cut in all types of jewelry, especially in engagement rings, making it easy to match with other jewelry. It has an incredible brilliance, like the round brilliant cut, but also has the advantage of accentuating long, slender finders. This shape optimizes carat weight, meaning that the drawn out and symmetrical shape can make it appear larger than round stones of a similar weight. The oval cut is also an ideal way to elongate shorter fingers and it has recently become fashionable to use as the center stone for engagement rings.

A "bow-tie effect" occurs when light passing through the diamond casts a shadow across the central facets of the stone. This shadow can be reduced by altering the depth of the pavilion and adjusting the angle of the table and facets to better diffuse light in the central area. This effect also occurs in the Pear, Marquise and Heart shapes.

Cushion Cut

Sometimes called a pillow-cut diamond, the cushion cut is a timeless cut that has earned its name for its pillow shape. Cushion cut diamonds tend to have impeccable brilliance and clarity in their appearance which can be attributed to their rounded corners and larger facets. These modified brilliants often have what is called the "sparkling water" or "crushed ice" effect, giving them greater scintillation. Because of its extra facets, the Cushion cut can disperse more light through the stone which serves to hide inclusions more efficiently, making it one of the most brilliant of all square- and rectangular-shaped stones. These diamonds are available in square and rectangular shapes.

Pear Shape

Combining round and marquise cuts, the teardrop style of pear-shaped diamonds is exceptional. The slender pear shape will give fingers and hands a slimmer appearance while creating a soft and delicate look. Pear shaped diamonds are cut to produce maximum brilliance, so it's important to look for excellent symmetry. Additionally, color is often more visible towards the tip of the pear shape, so to ensure an even tone throughout the stone it is advisable to opt for colors H and above.

Marquise Cut

A marquise cut diamond is a perfect shape for maximizing carat weight by emphasizing the size of the diamond. Its unique shape creates the effect of longer, more slender hands and fingers. The outline of a diamond is determined by its length to width ratio, which also provides an image of the shape and look of the diamond.

Emerald Cut

Emerald cut diamonds have a unique optical appearance because of the rectangular facets step-cut into the diamond's pavilion. This cut showcases the diamond's original clarity beautifully because of its large rectangular table which will also make inclusions and color more apparent.

Ascher Cut

Ascher cut diamonds are often mistaken for an emerald cut because of its similar cut style; however, an Ascher is square rather than rectangular. Created in the early 1920s, the Ascher cut has recently resurged in popularity, especially amongst celebrities.

Heart Cut

The exact origins of the heart brilliant are unknown although being a modified brilliant cut it may have appeared as early as the 16th century. While it is not a favorite of mine, it is popular amongst the romantics. When presenting a hear diamond throw in the phrase "Capture her heart… never let it go". It gets them every time. If you do not offer heart shaped diamonds tell your customer that the tip of Cupid's arrows aren't hearts, they are diamond. Then show them the side profile of a diamond. This is believed to be where our modern shape of a heart came from, so every diamond is a heart shape diamond.

THE FIFTH C

Once you understand the 4 C's it is easy to gain the 5th C. Confidence. You are an educated, helpful sales consultant who understands all there is to know about diamonds. You are going to help your customers find all that they could have ever hoped for through your presentation skills. Nothing inspires trust more than confidence. Be confident in the quality of jewelry you sell, company you represent, the service you provide. Be proud of your profession. We celebrate the most intimate occasions that few other people get to be a part of.

Fun Facts to tell your customers
• The ancient Greeks believed that diamonds were splinters of stars fallen to the earth.
• Only 500 tons of diamonds have ever been mined in recorded history to date.
• You must mine 629 tons of earth to yield one carat.
• Cupid's arrows are tipped with diamonds. That is where the heart shape comes from (look at the side profile of a diamond. Doesn't matter the shape they all have a heart on the side).
• The reason an engagement ring is worn on the third finger of the left-hand dates back to an ancient Egyptian belief that the vein of love (vena amoris) ran from the tip of the third finger and directly to the heart.
• Plato wrote about diamonds as living beings that embodied celestial spirits.
• Less than one percent of all women will ever wear a one carat diamond or more.
• The word diamond comes from the word adamas which means unconquerable and indestructible.

Knowing all these facts and figures are fantastic and are going to add a lot of firepower to your arsenal. However, the 4 c's and a well-known history are not going to sell your diamonds. How you use these to create and draw emotion is what is going to sell. Diamonds are built on emotion and it is the only emotion that is going to make your customer purchase a diamond.

Romance the gemstone.
Romance how well it is made.

Romance the gift giving moment.
Romance the occasion.
Romance future use.
Romance your store.
Romance your services.

The 4C's really don't have much to do with "good" or "bad." They're simply outcomes of the astonishing process through which Nature shaped each diamond's potential for beauty and value. Explaining this can help some customers overcome reservations about a diamond that has inclusions or a tint of color. For others it can underscore the rarity of large, high quality diamonds.

Compared to any other gem – indeed any other material that's known – diamond's properties are exceptional in every way. However, your customer doesn't know this, and not providing customers with adequate information to make an informed decision is the #1 reason customers walk away from purchasing items that they otherwise are interested in. Fixing this one thing will boost your sales significantly. It has waited billions of years for you to present the secrets of its beauty. Don't let it down.

CHAPTER 4: COLORED GEMSTONES

Quality is never an accident; it is always the result of high intention, sincere effort, intelligent direction and skillful execution; it represents the wise choice of many alternatives.
William A. Foster

The category of colored gemstones includes all significant gems that are not diamonds. Although they are very different, each have made their own mark on history. Colored gemstones are filled with romance, mystery, and come from the most remote regions of the world. Because of the sheer number of colored gemstones available I am only going to go over some of the most popular gemstones of all; birthstones. This knowledge is going to be a solid foundation for you to build on as you discover what gems are distinct to your store.

Birthstones

It is imperative that you memorize the birthstones. Would you buy a car from a car salesman that couldn't tell you the difference between car brands? It is the same in the jewelry world. Memorizing the birthstones will give you that little bridge of trust between you and your customer. They will believe that you are an oracle of information and will ask you questions freely. This flow of information then allows you to be in a position where you can guide them to a purchase that will have more meaning, make a bigger impact in their relationship, and put more money in your pocket.

Begin your gemstone journey by memorizing which birthstone is associated with which month of the year. Below is the modern list of birthstones for the United States of America. If you are operating outside the USA, you may have to do some research on your own as different countries have their own lists. Once you have gotten this basic knowledge down to a 'T' you can then take a deeper dive into how each birthstone has a place in many traditions, customs, and belief systems.

January:	Garnet
February:	Amethyst
March:	Aquamarine
April:	Diamond/White Topaz
May:	Emeralds
June:	Alexandrite/Pearl
July:	Ruby
August:	Peridot
September:	Sapphire
October:	Opal
November:	Citrine
December:	Blue Topaz/Tanzanite

But where did the idea of birthstones come from? Many historians and gemstone seeks alike believe that the origin of birthstones date back to the breastplate of Aaron worn some three millennia ago. The breastplate was of great religious significance and contained twelve gemstones. Roman scholar Titus Flavius Josephus in the first century A.D., who apart from having a fabulous name, studied the twelve gemstones of Aaron's

Breastplate, and connected the 12 stones to the 12 signs of the Zodiac. With that connection to the month of a person's birth, the jump from Zodiac stone to birth stone was a simple one. Since then, each stone has evolved over the centuries to have their own unique story.

Garnet

The word "garnet" comes from the 14th Century Middle English word "gernet" meaning dark red. The word is derived from Latin "granatum" which means seed and is called so because of the gemstone's resemblance to the beautiful red seeds of the pomegranate.

This stone symbolizes romantic love, passion and intimacy. Early explorers believed it would protect them from evil and disaster on dry land or as they sailed the high seas. It's said that Noah carried a Garnet lantern to steer the ark at night as it drudged the flooded earth. In Hinduism and Buddhism, garnet is seen as a holy stone that enlightens the soul and gives wisdom. Garnet symbolizes constructiveness and works best on the root and sacral chakras. In addition, mystics believe it brightens dark souls and brings hope to people.

Garnet is said to release negative energy. Anyone subject to depression should carry a tumbled garnet. Legend has it that the garnet can bring peace, prosperity and good health to the home. Some even called it the "Gem of Faith," and it's believed that those who wear it and do good, more good will come (conversely, it was also said to bring very bad fortune to those who commit bad acts while wearing it). The gemstone encourages the feeling of joy, willpower, and hope, while its fiery color drives away fatigue and stimulates the imagination.

Amethyst

For centuries amethyst was regarded as one of the five

cardinal gems. These were held to be the most valuable and rare of all gemstones. Large deposits, discovered during the 18th century in Brazil, made this coveted jewel more readily available for a gem hungry public. The name "amethyst" is derived from Greek, meaning "not drunken." According to Ancient Greek lore, the stone could ward off the intoxicating powers of Bacchus, the Roman god of wine and intoxication, and keep the wearer clear-headed and quick-witted. To this day, you can find drinking cups made from amethyst that were designed to protect oneself from drunkenness.

The color purple was traditionally the color of royalty, and amethyst was used to adorn the richest and most powerful monarchs and rulers. The English revered the stone for its majestic properties — creating emblems and insignia featuring amethysts during the Middle Ages to symbolize royalty. Amethyst is a member of the quartz family and is considered the most highly prized variety of quartz. In fact, Leonardo Da Vinci once wrote that amethyst quickens intelligence and gets rid of evil thoughts. thought to be helpful in overcoming addiction.

Aquamarine

March is a month of transitions. It is a month to welcome the bright colors of spring and a toast to a new beginning. A lot about March is extraordinary, including its gorgeous birthstone. For those born in this month have a perfect birthstone that is both beautiful and versatile. The serene aquamarine invokes the tranquility of its namesake, the sea. Derived from the Latin phrase "aqua marinus," meaning "water of the sea," aquamarine shimmers in ocean blues and greens.

Tying into its name, the aquamarine gemstone encapsulates all things connected to the sea. In ancient folklore, this blue gem was believed to be a treasure of mermaids and was used by sailors for protection, good luck, fearlessness, and safety while at sea. To this day, aquamarine is used to protect those who travel by, over or near water. Therefore, wearing aquamarine while flying internationally or taking a cruise could keep the wearer's mind at ease.

Aquamarine was first discovered in India more than 2,000 years ago. Since then, people have credited both paranormal and mystical properties to it. In the Middle Ages, many believed that the simple act of wearing aquamarine was a natural antidote to poisoning. The Sumerians, Egyptians, and Hebrews all admired aquamarine, and many warriors would wear it on the battlefield to bring about victory. Many ancient medicines used powder from aquamarine to help cure all manners of infection, but it was said to be particularly beneficial for eye ailments.

However, the stone only became popular after larger samples from Brazil surfaced in the market in 1910. 43 years later, in 1953 Brazil gifted an aquamarine and diamond necklace with matching pendant and earrings to Queen Elizabeth II as a coronation gift. It took an entire year to gather and perfectly match the stones. The queen loved the gift so much that she commissioned a matching tiara in 1957.

Aquamarine is a calming stone which is said to bring peace, inspire trust, and facilitates honest communication. This gem is also supposed to help people overcome the fear of speaking, making it a perfect gift choice for the family and friends that are teachers or presenters.

Diamond
You have an entire chapter dedicated to diamonds; you better know enough by now to sell diamonds to every

single birthday in April. They are the lucky ones since all their jewelry will be diamond based and always match!

Blue and White Topaz

Topaz is from the Greek word "topazion" which stems from the Sanskrit "tapas" meaning fire. Considered as "The Colored Gemstone", because of the incredible variety of colors available! Topaz is frequently available as a colorless stone, and it is often employed as an accent stone in lieu of diamonds. Its hardy and colorless nature also lend it to treatment. Topaz can be heat-treated to create jewels such as London Blue and Electric Blue varieties. Alternatively, vapor deposition creates gorgeous gems like the many varieties of Mystic Topaz seen on the market.

Topaz has a long and often times disputed history, primarily because it has been confused with other minerals many times. For thousands of years, before gemologists and geologists could differentiate between minerals, all golden colored gemstones were called topaz. For instance, gems like golden citrine and smokey quartz and even peridot were considered to be topaz even though they are entirely different minerals. It's easy to understand why because to the naked eye, it is nearly impossible to tell the difference between golden citrine and a similarly colored topaz.

Red and pink topaz gems were used in the jewelry of the 18th and 19th Century Russian Czarinas and is why topaz is sometimes called "Imperial Topaz".

Topaz is a relatively hard stone, making it a great choice for jewelry you will be wearing every day. It rates 8 on the Mohs hardness scale and is fairly resistant to scratching. Not only is it physically tough, but it makes your tougher. During the Middle Ages topaz was thought to heal both physical and mental disorders. In some cases, larger crystals were said to prevent death. Even before then the Greeks believed it had power to increase strength and to make its wearer invisible while the Romans believed it had power to improve eyesight. The Egyptians wore it as an amulet to protect them from injury.

This gem can do just about anything because it has been confused as other gems all throughout history.

Emerald

Similar to the naming of the infamous ruby, emerald's first name was "smaragdus", the ancient Greek word for green. Rome's Pliny the Elder published in the first century AD where he described emeralds: "…nothing greens greener" was his verdict. He described the use of emerald by early lapidaries, who "have no better method of restoring their eyes than by looking at the emerald, its soft, green color comforting and removing their weariness and lassitude." Funny enough, 2000 years later, modern technology has proven that the color green is known to relieve stress and eye strain.

Emerald green is one of the most vibrant and expressive of colored gemstones. It is intoxicating in its charm. Ireland is the Emerald Isle. Seattle, in the US state of Washington, is the Emerald City. Thailand's most sacred religious icon is called the Emerald Buddha, even though it's carved from green jadeite. All of these use emeralds in their name to borrow its history and become more alluring. What is more compelling to see than emerald?

The first known emerald mines were in Egypt, operating from before 330 BC and continued to be into service into the late 1700's. Cleopatra was one of the most famous conesours of those very emeralds. Near the end of the Egyptian mine's life emeralds from what is now Colombia were part of the plunder when sixteenth-century Spanish explorers invaded the New World. The Incas had already been using emeralds in their jewelry and religious ceremonies for 500 years. The Spanish, who treasured gold and silver far more than gems, traded emeralds for precious metals. Their trades opened the eyes of European and Asian royalty to the emerald's majesty.

It didn't take much for emerald to become the most famous member of the beryl family. Since its discovery legends sprang up left and right. It endowed the wearer with the ability to foresee the future when emerald was placed under the tongue. It could reveal truth and be protected against evil spells. Emerald was once even believed to cure diseases like cholera and malaria. Wearing an emerald was believed to reveal the truth or falseness of a lover's oath as well as make one an eloquent speaker. Legend also states that emerald was one of the four precious stones given by God to King Solomon. These four stones were said to have endowed the king with power over all creation.

Whether these stories were used to try to give reasoning to an unusually brilliant stone or there is some actual mystical element involved we will never know. What we do know is that emeralds are a part of the beryl family and that they are quite distinguishable from any other gem. Most emeralds are highly included, so their toughness (resistance to breakage) is classified as generally poor.

Pearls

Pearls were the first gems coveted by prehistoric people. Found purely by chance while opening shells for food, early humans were easily enchanted by the luminous glow emanating from these gifts of the sea. It wasn't long before pearls became the gem of choice for the highest echelons of societies. The monetary value of pearls restricted ownership of them throughout history. Only kings, queens and other elites could afford them. In many societies ownership was even restricted by law. Pearls are even mentioned in the Talmud and the Bible.

These echelons of society have even passed on a legend published by Pliny the Elder between two of the highest echelons society has ever had to offer the world. Cleopatra, Queen of the Ancient Egyptian and Marc Antony, one of the most pivotal politicians of the Roman empire. The legend describes a wager between the two in 41 B.C. where Cleopatra bet that she could host the most expensive feasts in history. Later, as the banquet began winding down Antony said that it was a fine meal but was not the most lavish meal he himself had ever participated in.

But Cleopatra was not finished. She reached up and removed one of her pearl earrings. The pearl was so large and rare that its documented worth was 10,000,000 sesterces, or the value of fifteen countries—a true fortune and dropped it into a goblet of wine. It was crushed, dissolved and Cleopatra drank it. The value of that single glass alone cemented it as the most expensive banquet in history.

Pearl diving was once the prime industry in the Persian Gulf and in many areas of Asia and the Americas. Like gold in the California Gold Rush of 1848, when a new pearl bed was discovered, it was promptly combed over until nearly all shells were thoroughly depleted. Millions of shells were collected with hopes of finding the elusive pearl, decimating shell populations around the world. But this all changed with the technical innovation and vision of one man near the turn of the twentieth century—Kokichi Mikimoto.

Many centuries ago, someone whose identity is lost to pearling history declared that a natural pearl forms when foreign matter, such as a grain of sand, invades a shelled mollusks soft tissue, and the mollusk progressively coats the invader with shell material to sooth the irritation it causes. That explanation has been repeated so often, it's taken as true. But both common sense and close analysis demonstrate it's false.

Pearls do not form around a grain of sand. Most often, pearls form around a small bit of organic matter or are a result of damage to the shell or the mantle muscle.

The finest strands emanate a glow rarely found in other cultured pearl varieties, which is one reason akoya pearls are still considered the gold standard in cultured pearl jewelry. People familiar with akoya pearls have likely heard of the legendary Kokichi Mikimoto. His story is so intertwined with this industry that "Mikimoto" is practically synonymous with "cultured pearls."

Black pearls burst into the limelight in the early 1970s, after being relatively unknown in most of the world. They were first viewed with skepticism, but quickly became a symbol of status and prestige. Elizabeth Taylor and other Hollywood elite draped themselves with strands of these dark exotic beauties, starting a new era of cultured pearl love. The term "black pearl" is a misnomer, as the pearls are rarely black. They come in a rainbow of different body colors and overtones. The finest pearls can hardly be described as black, exhibiting dark green and blue colors, with iridescent overtones of rose and gold.

Dark, colorful pearls from the islands of Tahiti are considered by many to be the most exotic of all cultured pearls. Tahitian pearls grow naturally in nearly every color imaginable, from white to charcoal black. The most common body colors are gray and green, but other colors such as copper, pistachios and dark blue are prevalent. Overtones such as peacock, purple, green, blue and even gold are common in Tahitian pearls and signal fine nacre quality. Intense peacock overtones show as a colorful shimmer, which remains stationary as a pearl is moved and turned. Tahitian pearls exhibiting this optical phenomenon are highly valued.

Alexandrite

Often considered to be 'emerald by day, ruby by night,' this moderately new gem, alexandrite was found in the Russian mines of the Ural Mountains in 1843. Folktales state that this color changing gemstone was discovered on the same day when future Russian Czar Alexander II was born. So naturally, this gemstone was named in honor of him. As this unique gem changes its color from green to red, Alexandrite enjoys the position as the official gemstone of Russia.

Alexandrite is also the rarest and the most valuable of all other gemstones owing to its qualities and its availability as well. Russia, the land where alexandrite gemstones were first found has not been producing these gemstones for quite some time. The stones are now sourced from other countries such as Brazil, India, Madagascar and Srilanka. However, Russian alexandrites were considered superior in quality.

The gemstone is considered to bring love, good luck and fortune. Since it is considered as a gemstone that promotes romance (the thing that Russians are famous for apparently), it is used as the centerpiece for engagement rings all across the globe.

It was also considered traveler's gem. It was believed to

help the wearer adapt to a new atmosphere, discern the principles of life of other cultures and find a way out to converse easily with those with a foreign tongue. It was believed that carrying this gemstone aided the owner in understanding other languages easily.

Ruby

Rubies bring to mind a deep shade of red similar to the blood that many have spilled in their search for it. Thousands of years ago the word ruby itself was born from the Latin word "ruber" which means red. Even in present times the brightest and most valuable shade of red called blood-red or pigeon blood commands a large premium over other rubies of similar quality. In most cases, ruby isn't the famously deep shade that comes to mind. Rubies can come in any color from light pink to the famous dark ruby red. The red color is lighter or darker depending on a ruby's level of chromium.

It might also surprise you to find out that ruby and sapphire come from the same genetic background. Both sapphires and rubies are formed from an element called corundum. The only difference between the two genetically is their color. This means that Rubies have a hardness of 9.0 on the Mohs scale of mineral hardness and are only beat out by diamonds.

With this information in mind, many of you will wonder, "Well what is a pink sapphire then?". In the United States of America, a minimum color saturation must be met to be called a ruby; otherwise, the stone will be classified as a pink sapphire. This helps keep rubies up to the deeply red standard that has held the hearts of consumers for centuries and not allow fraud men to sell pink sapphires on the market as rubies and dilute the value of their genuine counterparts.

When it comes to legend, many societies value rubies as mystical artifacts that allow bearers of the gemstone to have better communication with God. Archaeologists have discovered rubies that were laid beneath the foundation of buildings to secure good fortune to the structure.

Peridot

We know peridot for its eye-catching lime green glow, and it is the modern August birthstone. Peridot is a French word that is derived from the Arabic word "faridat" meaning gem. This jewel is the rare gem-quality of the mineral olivine (also referred to as chrysolite) which occurs deep inside the planet. Natural processes of the earth like volcanoes bring this gorgeous gem to the planet's surface. So, wherever there are or were volcanoes, this mineral is likely to be found. In Hawaii, the stone is involved in ancient folklore and is said to symbolize the tears of the Goddess Pele, the goddess of volcanoes and fire.

The use of peridot in jewelry and other applications dates as far back as the ancient Egyptians from around 1500 B.C., making it one of the oldest recognizable gemstones. In ancient times, Egypt was the primary source of the peridot, called the 'Gem of the Sun'. The Egyptians were extremely fascinated with the peridot, and they were made into Talisman to ward off evil. Many argue that the gemstones worn by Queen Cleopatra was not emeralds as it was popularly believed, but the peridot. Travelers at the time were not yet familiar with the rare stone and may have mistook it for the darker green gemstone they already knew.

Peridot is thought to aid in the success of marriage and other relationships. This may be because it is thought to encourage positive energy as well as suppress ego and jealousy. Romans referred to peridot as "evening emerald" because unlike the deep hues of emeralds, peridot gemstones did not darken at night and still shimmered under candlelight.

Sapphire

One of the most prominent and popular colored gemstones in history, sapphires have been on top of the world for millennia. They have been sought after by kings, noblemen and treasure hunters since their first discovery. They were so desired that the oldest gem in the British Crown Jewels is a sapphire that belonged to King Edward the Confessor (he reigned in the 11th century and died in 1066). Even the world's most famous engagement ring had a sapphire in place of a diamond: Kate Middleton and Princess Diana's sapphire.

Sapphires are sought after because of their rich beauty and the lore surrounding them. Along with its uniquely mesmerizing deep shades of blue, sapphires were also coveted for their mystical powers. In ancient Roman times, kings wore them for protection from danger in both battle and political situations. Many historians believe that this is because sapphires themselves are extremely resilient.

Compared to diamonds -the hardest natural substance on earth- sapphires follow closely behind being a 9 on the Mohs hardness scale. This makes sapphires excellent jewelry pieces because of their ability to take a beating.

Opal

In 75 AD Roman scholar Pliny observed, "Some opali carry such a play within them that they equal the deepest and richest colors of painters. Others…simulate the flaming fire of burning sulphur and even the bright blaze of burning oil." He marveled that this kaleidoscopic gem encompassed the red of ruby, the green of emerald, the yellow topaz, the blue of sapphire, and the purple of amethyst.

The name opal originates from the Roman word "opalus" which traces its roots from the Greek's "opallios" meaning to see a change of color. This Greek word is likewise a revision of the ancient Indian Sanskrit's "upala" which means precious stone. These stones display an incredible play of light across their surface, as they enchant with the myriad of colors they can display. Also known as "Queen of Gems," no two opals are alike.

Arabic legends say it falls from the heavens in flashes of lightning. The ancient Greeks believed opals gave their owners the gift of prophecy and guarded them from disease. Europeans have long considered the gem a symbol of hope, purity, and truth. Opal has been regarded as the luckiest and most magical of all gems because it can show all colors.

Opal is also one of the most unique forming gemstones. Unlike most other gems that formed from extreme heat and pressure, opals came to be in the reverse. While diamonds are formed in huge lava caverns, opals are the handiwork of seasonal rains. These rainstorms drenched dry ground in regions such as Australia's famous "outback" desert. The rainwater soaked deep into ancient underground rock, dissolving silica (a compound of silicon and oxygen) and carrying it downward.

Later, dry periods would again evaporate much of the water that had fallen leaving large caches of silica in the cracks and between the layers of underground sedimentary rock. Over thousands of years, these silica deposits materialized into opal.

Opal is most famously known for its unique exhibit of candescent rainbow colors. We call this play-of-color. There are two broad classes of opal: precious and common. Precious opal displays play-of-color, common opal does not.

Play-of-color occurs in precious opal because it's made up of sub-microscopic spheres stacked in a grid-like pattern—like layers of Ping-Pong balls in a box. As the light waves travel between the spheres, the waves diffract, or bend. As they bend, they break up into the colors of the rainbow, called spectral colors. Play-of-color is the result.

Citrine
Citrine was announced as the official November birthstone in 1912 by The Jewelers of America. Citrine is a yellow variety of quartz displaying hues ranging from pale yellow to brown. The stunning color of the gem is due to the ferric or iron impurities found in its structure. It is recognized as one of the most popular and frequently purchased yellow gemstones.

For those who love the yellow and orange of Imperial Topaz, Citrine is a great alternative. From the lemon yellows of Brazilian Citrine to the deep red orange of Madeira Citrine, it's easy to find your favorite stone. One of the best qualities of this beautiful stone is its affordability! Even fine citrine doesn't cost an arm and a leg. Price per carat doesn't rise dramatically for larger sizes, so even the large stones remain affordable. It's hard to believe that such a gorgeous stone won't break the bank.

Citrine is believed to be of value in healing the spiritual self as well, as it is a powerful cleanser and regenerator. It carries the virtues of self-healing, inspiration and self-improvement. Carrying the power of the sun, it is excellent for overcoming depression, fears and phobias. It aids those with a depressed self-esteem. One's sense of self becomes more radiant with a citrine and it helps to look forward to the future optimistically, going with the flow, instead of hanging on to the past. With the traditional colors of yellow and orange, the modern November birthstones are an excellent way to inject a burst of happy color all year long.

Tanzanite

A relatively new gemstone, tanzanite is the blue to violet variety of zoisite. Described as 'a geological phenomenon', tanzanite is 1,000 times rarer than diamonds and is only found in one place: a 4km (2.49 miles) strip of land in the Merelani Foothills of Tanzania. Gemologists believe that it is unlikely to ever be found anywhere else, and in the next 10 to 20 years no new tanzanite will be available to the market. After it becomes depleted, there won't be any more first-time owners of the gem, and all tanzanite will become precious heirlooms.

Popular for displaying a transition of color from blue to violet, with flashes of red, tanzanite exhibits pleochroism, meaning that the color of the gemstone shifts as you change its position. Tanzanite is uniquely trichroic. This means that in its rough form, it radiates three different colors from each of its crystallographic axes: blue, violet and red. Once cut and polished, tanzanite ranges from electric violets to vibrant blues, deep royals and rich indigos. Also, this gemstone is believed to boost the immune system, communication skills, and sharpen the mind. Tanzanite is becoming increasingly recognized as an heirloom due to its very limited supply and rarity.

CHAPTER 5: RING MATERIALS

Quality is never an accident; it is always the result of high intention, sincere effort, intelligent direction and skillful execution; it represents the wise choice of many alternatives.
William A. Foster

Precious metals have played a unique role in human history. Explorers have set out across the world in search for them discovering entirely new continents for trade and commerce in the process. Whether used for ornamental purposes, talismans to ward off evil, or to be used as currency we simply can't get enough.

Gold
For thousands of years gold has been the stuff of legends. It has been lusted after by kings and treasure hunters alike. It has been stamped and traded as currency in ancient times and in more current times has been transformed into the standard backing of our monetary system. In the Olympics it is used as a sign of complete victory and is now integral to our modern way of life with it being necessary for our phones to work.

To go back to its original roots, we must look as far

back as 4,600 B.C. where archaeologists believe that man first began mining for gold. Since then, gold has earned its very own spot on the periodic table where its atomic symbol is Au. Au comes from the Greek word "aurum", which means "glow of sunshine" and is used for the name of a sweet Italian liqueur. Isn't that just the most romantic thing?

Gold has an allure because of that unique yellow shine. The English word gold comes from the Latin word "geolu" which means yellow. It gets this enchanting shine because its unique arrangement of electrons. This special subatomic arrangement is also what makes gold one of the most optimal materials for jewelry wear.

Firstly, Gold is the most malleable and ductile of all metals. This makes it optimal for us to be able to shape gold into any number of imaginable jewelry pieces. One ounce of gold can be stretched into almost 50 miles (80 km) of thin gold wire. That same ounce of gold can be beaten into a sheet covering 9 square miles and be only 0.000018 cm thick.

Gold is also useful in jewelry because it does not oxidize or rust in any way. This is the attribute that makes jewelry so timeless. The same ring that your great-great-great grandmother wore will still look presentable after years of everyday wear.

Along with those fantastic characteristics that make gold such a useful and desired metal there is something else that adds to its value. Gold is one of the scarcest of metals. It is estimated that the entire supply of gold of the planet equals a total of 168,180 tons or 5,407,112,558 ounces. To visualize this volume, let's imagine a single solid gold cube with edges of about 19 meters. That means that the entire supply of gold available on earth is about three meters shorter than the length of a tennis court. You are more likely to find a five-carat diamond than you are to find a one-ounce nugget of gold.

Since gold is so scarce, measuring gold needs to be a precise system so that its value can be maximized. Today we use an ancient recipe that has changed very little over millennia - the karat system. This ancient recipe is based on 24 equal parts. Pure gold is 24 parts gold and is written as 24 karat or 24k gold. A different mixture could be 18 parts gold and 6 parts some other material which would make 18k gold. 14 parts gold with 10 parts other metals is 14k gold and so on.

A more modern approach used by most international jewelry manufacturers use a metric-type fineness system that's based on parts per thousand. Under this system, 750 is the same as 18K. This is because 750/1000 and 18/24 both equal 0.75, or 75%. Most other metric markings also match up with standard karat ratings.

While gold ranges anywhere from 5k to pure 24k gold, you will mostly work in the 10-18k range. Some designer pieces will use 20, 22 or 24k as an accent color but almost never for the entire piece. This is because the higher carat alloys are much too soft so survive normal wear and tear. Only experienced jewelry enthusiasts should consider having any of the higher ranged designer pieces. Just because a jewelry piece isn't pure gold doesn't mean that it is any less valuable, but because there is less gold this will also bring the price down. The other upside is that the less gold that there is in a ring, the stronger and more durable the ring will become. The optimal balance that achieves both durability and shine is 14k golds.

Along with being different levels of gold in each ring, you also have different colors of gold to choose from.

Gold rings are available in a variety of colors from a cool bronze to a lively green. The most popular colors are yellow gold, rose gold and white gold. Don't be confused, all gold comes out of the ground in its natural, rich yellow color. To make rose and white gold the gold is then mixed with other alloys to create new eye-catching colors. Increasing the copper ratio creates pink to rose red, while upping the proportion of silver results in green. White gold usually includes palladium – a metal related to platinum – plus zinc and sometimes nickel. Any other colors you carry will be made from special techniques unique to each manufacturer.

Because of these different combinations of metals some will require regular maintenance and others will not. Yellow gold and rose gold are permanent. Even after years of wear and tear a simple cleaning and polishing can restore a ring to its original glory. White gold needs a little more love and care. With time, the white gold shine on will wear off to reveal the natural yellow of gold underneath. It is nothing to be concerned about and is completely reversible. All that is required to return it to its natural, original white gold self is a process known as rhodium dipping. It is a non-invasive, simple process that only takes a day or so to complete. The number of times that you will need to get your ring rhodium dipped varies from person to person. Some people go most of their lives without ever needing it while others are more frequent. On average you will only need to repeat this process every 2.5 years.

Silver

Silver is chosen for jewelry mainly because of is historical popularity. Once it was discovered by our ancestors it was immediately deemed to be a precious material because of its natural beauty. However, it is the demand for silver that has created the sales arena, not its properties. In ancient Egypt, silver was less common than gold and was therefore deemed to be much more valuable. Silver's cool crisp color is one of its chief attractions. While "weight" is a selling point for the other metals, "lightness" makes silver perfect for big bold designs that would otherwise be too heavy to wear comfortably.

Like the other precious metals, silver is alloyed for jewelry purposes. Most US manufacturers use sterling silver, which is 92.5% silver and 7.5% copper. The recipe for sterling silver was developed in England during the 1300s, and it's harder and tougher than pure silver.

However, you need to know the properties of silver because many of your customers may ask you to set their grandmother's diamond in silver. Silver makes beautiful jewelry but because of its unique properties shouldn't be your first choice for settings:

• Silver is not as strong as 9ct Gold or Platinum.
• It will tarnish after a period of time - other precious metals do not.
• May cause an allergic reaction in some wearers.

By knowing silver's properties, you can now inform your customer that setting their grandmother's diamond in silver may be dangerous. Here is a conversation that you may have with a customer that you have built a good rapport with.

Salesman: "Your ring is beautiful; would you like me to polish it for free today?"

Cameron: "Thank you, it is my grandmother's ring. I was wondering if it would be possible to take out her center diamond and put it in a new silver ring? Can you do that?"

Salesman: "Of course we can! Why did you choose silver?"

Cameron: "I like the silver color. It matches my style."

Salesman: "Silver is a beautiful color, but I worry that it won't be strong enough to protect your grandmother's diamond. I want you to be able to pass on your ring for generations, and gold is going to be stronger, more durable, and hold its shine longer."

If you are trying to sell a customer on a gold setting versus a silver, gold is much denser than silver giving it some heft. Many customers will associate weight with value, so if you can find two similarly designed silver and gold rings you can have customers hold them both, so they understand that gold is better quality by feeling it for themselves.

Silver VS Gold

Gold and silver are the most popular of the precious metals, largely because they function very well in a similar number of ways, especially in terms of decorative purposes. Each of the precious metals is rare, they are perfect for making jewelry, and they are both rather sturdy, so why is gold more expensive and why should you always try to sell diamond rings in gold?

One of the most crucial elements that go into making silver less expensive than gold is the rarity of the metal itself. Gold is simply rarer than silver – much rarer – and this imbalance in supply and demand between the two metals makes up most of the difference in their prices. For example, if it large gold ores were discovered tomorrow that made gold more plentiful than silver, it's likely that gold would see a drastic drop in price, especially if suddenly gold becomes more plentiful than even silver. For example, after the discovery of the New World, silver was so plentiful for the Spanish Empire that it caused rapid silver inflation, having an unforeseen negative impact on the economy. However, such a dramatic change is unlikely to occur.

Gold is also more durable than sterling silver. It is more scratch-resistant, and it doesn't tarnish. Both gold and silver are durable, however, because they are both precious metals. Sterling silver is 92.5 percent pure silver and 7.5 percent metal alloy. This metal alloy makes sterling silver durable enough for daily wear, but it isn't something you should trust to hold diamonds or large precious stones. Gold also requires less maintenance. Both sterling silver jewelry and gold jewelry should be cleaned regularly, but silver jewelry tarnishes over time requiring it to be polished occasionally. Wearing silver jewelry every day helps keep the tarnish at bay but leave it off for too long and it will get a gross gray coating on its surface. Silver cleaner (that usually smells super gross) and a soft cloth will remove tarnish easily, but very few people know about it. Gold jewelry can be cleaned with warm, soapy water or polished with a jewelry cloth making it much easier to maintain.

Platinum

The first wave of platinum popularity occurred in the early 1900's, but quickly ended with World War II (1939-1945). Because of the war, the US government declared platinum a strategic material and removed it from the consumer market. The government took this step because platinum has many scientific and industrial uses. While the metal was off the market, this is when white gold crept in and gained favor as an alternative. Since then, white gold hasn't let go of what it took and has been more popular.

Platinum is often used in purer forms than gold. As you've seen, karat gold normally ranges from about 42% pure (with 10K) to 75% pure (with 18K). Platinum's fineness is measured in parts per thousand, and much of the platinum jewelry manufactured in the US is 900 or 950 platinum. That means it's 90% or 95% pure.

Along with platinum being purer, likewise, it is far more expensive to purchase. Platinum is one of the rarest metals in the world. So rare, in fact, that all the platinum ever mined would fit into your living room. Combine that with its unique shine and sheer then you have a luxurious metal worth top dollar.

Derived from the Spanish term "platino", meaning "little silver" platinum is naturally "white" in color. This color does not fade or tarnish – it keeps its natural white color forever. Platinum is not only beautiful; it is also robust. When gold is scratched a piece of gold is torn off the ring. With platinum a scratch merely causes a displacement of the metal, with no loss of its volume. Platinum is 3x denser than gold; and Platinum jewelry is made of 95% pure metal. Platinum is one of the least reactive metals and it is as hypoallergenic as can be.

MEN's METALS
Tungsten
Easily the most asked for and talked about men's ring material is tungsten. The reason for that is because it is around 10 times harder than 18k gold and 4 times as hard as titanium. This is one of the biggest selling points. Tungsten can take a beating for years and look much newer than just about any other men's ring. This doesn't make it scratch proof, but tougher than the rest.

Another big selling factor is the weight. Tungsten is denser than other metals and while this allows it to be very strong, it also makes it very heavy. Men they will like having the extra weight on their hands for two reasons:

1. It makes it feel more secure on their hand.
2. Weight is tied to value. The heavier it is the better-

quality things seem.

Titanium

Quite the opposite of tungsten, but still rough and tough, a ring made of titanium will weigh around a fifth of the same sized ring made of its cousin tungsten, and around a quarter of the weight of a ring fashioned from gold. Titanium is the metal to choose for those who do not want to feel like they are wearing a ring at all. Its light, incredibly scratch resistant and is popular amongst first time wearers.

Have your customers try on both a tungsten and titanium ring when they are beginning their jewelry search. Ask them if they like the lighter or heavier men's rings. This is a good place to start their search.

Ceramic

Ceramic rings are some of the least expensive materials, but don't let that fool you. While it can be made from fired clay, most are more often formed from high-tech ceramics such as tungsten carbide and titanium carbide. So, don't let the name foot you, unlike the ceramic used to make your favorite vase, these rings are shatter resistant. Not only are they tough, they're by far the most heat-resistant of the men's ring materials. They are so effective that NASA uses the same material as heat-deflectors for their Space to Earth re-entry vehicles.

Electricians are going to swoon over these. They have all seen what happens when a buddy of theirs touches the wrong wire and gets their ring branded into their skin. Oftentimes to combat this they buy cheap silicone bands from amazon. You, however, are going to know a little secret.

whispers Ceramic rings don't conduct electricity.

That means that they can now have something to better express themselves with! New wives want their man to have something nice on his finger. Tell her that this is going to be something he can put on once and never take off because it is safe and fashionable. They will buy from you then and there.

These benefits are not just limited to electricians either. Any job that requires heavy machinery runs the risk of their hands being crushed. Ceramic rings won't pinch off a finger like a gold band and will instead break. These have been the difference between having a ten fingered husband and a nine fingered husband.

These unique attributes can be used to sell anyone but is especially effective on more sensitive/picky customers. Ceramic rings are completely allergenic free for those with unique allergies and they come in a variety of colors, patterns and textures to appease even your most nitpicky customers. You can sell these all day long.

SETTINGS

Now that you know about the very essence of what rings are made of, let's start looking at how they can be worn. Gemstones can be set in any number of ways and while we cannot go over every possible way that diamonds are set, we are going to go over the most popular settings. Not only will you learn what they are, but you will discover new ways of thinking about describing them to your customers.

When you describe a setting, for most, this will be the very first time they have ever seen or heard of the setting. Some can't even fathom that there are multiple ways for a diamond to be held on a finger. Your job is to inform, present and spray a little magic on each presentation as you move them towards a close. When describing a setting, don't just hold a setting up to their face and say, "this is a solitaire in a prong setting". Add the romance that they are looking for and then tack on the benefits that they need. Namely, security.

Below are examples that you can use to introduce an individual setting to a customer when they see if for the first time.

Prong Setting – In this type of setting, slender golden claws hold the gem. This style can raise the gem above the body of the jewelry, making it stand out and dramatizing it. Prong settings are favorites for transparent gemstones because they help capture as much light as possible allowing for maximum bedazzlement while still holding its jewel securely.

Bezel Setting – A metal collar/rim surrounds the gem and wraps slightly over its outer edge. Because the gem is partially covered it will usually appear somewhat smaller than it would in a prong setting, but it's held securely and is one of the most well protected settings you can ask for.

Cluster Setting – A number of gems are set close together, most often in a geometric or floral pattern. These settings allow you to have the look of a much larger center at a fraction of the cost. It's ideal for everyday wear because the gems are individually secured by small prongs or bezels for maximum hold.

Channel Setting – This style typically features rows of small gems set side-by-side between parallel ridges of gold. These diamonds were designed for this ring specifically because in order to be channel set, the gems must be cut to the same dimensions. These diamonds were destined to be together, just like you and your partner, and they will be together forever because of how tightly you hold on to each other.

RINGS

You got the basics of describing how rings are set, now it's time to know how to describe the rings themselves. Band – A ring that's relatively uniform in width and thickness. Bands are often used as wedding rings. They range from plain metal to very ornate designs that include gems, but the gems and their settings normally don't stand out from the body of the ring. Solitaire Ring – A band of precious metal with a single gemstone in a prominent setting. The diamond solitaire is the most popular choice for engagement rings, but there are countless variations for gems of all kinds. Closely related styles feature small diamonds or colored gems as accents flanking a large center gemstone.

Halo Ring – This has a large central gem circled by a single row of smaller gems. The halo both accents the center diamond and creates a circle of protection for the center diamond.

Three-Diamond Ring – A style that has three diamonds of about the same size in a line across the finger. (Sometimes the center diamond is a little larger than the other two.) Symbolizing the past, present, and future of a relationship, meaning I've loved you then, I especially love you now (if its bigger), and I am going to love you forever.

Two Stone – Two stone diamond rings were designed with special attention to symbolism. One stone represents you and the other represents your true love. A fun spin is to show it to a customer and tell them that one stone symbolizes your best friend, the other stone symbolizes your true love and you are giving it to the person who is both *immediately swoons*.

Eternity Ring – A ring set with a complete circle of small diamonds or colored gems. This is another popular choice for weddings and anniversaries. However, of all the rings there are some concerns that you should let your customer know about. For example, there isn't a single person in the world whose finger size isn't going to change and guess what? Eternity rings cannot be sized. Also, it is important that you tell them that some customers have issues with the diamonds rubbing against their skin. You want your customers to wear their jewelry forever, not sitting on a shelf in the closet. You don't want to spend all that money and have that happen. You want to wear your jewelry forever, don't you?

Right-Hand Ring – A non-bridal ring (meaning not for an engagement or wedding) that's worn on the right hand. It usually features at least one fairly large gemstone, but there are many design variations for this style. For many they are reminders of loved ones, past memories and special occasions.

WARDROBING

The beauty of there being so many kinds of settings is that customers can have a different ring for each style. Today's jewelry offers a constantly changing and expanding selection of beauty and style. You must show a customer how to accessorize with jewelry — how to wear it in different ways and in different combinations to express herself. You need to awaken them to the concept of wardrobing. Wardrobing is the art of choosing what jewelry to wear, what occasions to have jewelry for, and what order to buy it in. The idea is simple and fairly intuitive: Start with the basics, and then add pieces for special occasions, to compliment a favorite outfit or to simply enlarge a personal collection. For example, a ring, stud earrings, and a solitaire pendant or necklace form the foundation for any diamond jewelry wardrobe. Versatile yet elegant, these are appropriate for wear any time or place. Possibilities for additional wardrobe items are as varied as the moments they celebrate.

As a sales professional, it's important for you to recognize that wardrobing isn't a single-presentation event. Instead, it's an ongoing – you might say "life-long" – process. Open your customers' eyes to all the options that they have available. Show them how good a new engagement ring looks with diamond studded earrings. Always be combining pieces so that your customers fall in love with the entire set, and not just one piece. You will make them feel like royalty as your dress them in diamonds from head to toe.

Use Your Knowledge

It's time to take all that you have learned and combine it with your sales presentation. No longer are you going to just pick up a ring and hand it to a person. You are going to present them with a history, tell them a story, educate them on the wonderful artwork pieces you are gently holding in your fingers. Then, you are going to pair it with an equally beautiful set of earrings or a necklace to complete a look.

Dazzle. Don't tell. When you are describing the setting of a ring avoid words that sound technical. This is a magical moment and so the way you describe your jewelry should be too. Here are a couple of examples that you can use:

- It's a band, not a shank,
- It's a crown, not a head.
- It's a setting, not a mounting (mountings are for walls)
- It's a shoulder, not a shank

- They're accent diamonds, not side stones (side stones are cheap)
- It's a Tiffany mounting, not a six prong.
- It's a guard, not an insert

Not only can you make the structure of a ring more appealing, but because of your product knowledge you subconsciously now have five areas of focus that you can use to sell your jewelry pieces.

•Aesthetic Appeal – Whether the design of a piece is classic or contemporary, it has aesthetic appeal. In other words, it's beautiful. The overall proportioning is attractive. The various elements are harmonious in size and style. They're also properly balanced and aligned. Use the very look of a piece to sell it. Only some of the time they will love how it looks and that will be enough for them to purchase. Usually you need to reinforce the aesthetic appeal of a ring with the next four areas of selling before you can close a deal.

- Construction – All of the components fit together. The piece is well constructed, and strong enough for its intended wear. There are no cracks or areas of weakness (like a ring shank that's so thin it can be easily bent). Talk about your rings as the tough nuts these are. When you hand a ring to a customer ask them to feel the weight. Tell them how a ring with that much weight will last for generations. If they prefer lighter rings, tell them how the craftsmanship has evolved over thousands of years to produce the material that allows for everyday wear without the weight interfering.

- Mechanical Function – Any mechanical parts function as they should. Clasps open and close properly, and they're strong enough to hold for years. The joints or hinges on a bracelet operate smoothly, and the safety catch or chain is in good working order. Highlight how easy it is to use and allow them to try for themselves.

• Finish – The surface of the piece is entirely polished or textured. Decorative finish patterns are distinct, evenly executed, and clearly demarcated. There are no rough spots, pits, scratches, or discolored areas. The inside or back of the piece is finished just as well as the top or front. Use these small details to show that your pieces aren't just thrown together willy-nilly. Expert craftsmen have dedicated their lives to giving them the best jewelry possible. This is the stuff that will get attention from across the room

• Setting – The setting (if there is one) is precise and secure. It displays the gem(s) attractively yet provides protection (though some setting styles are naturally more protective than others). In group settings, all the gems are even, aligned, and properly oriented. Use the setting to ease the minds of those who have heard the horror stories of couples losing their diamonds. Your product is designed to last as long as possible and the setting is going to help them do just that. Few things ease the minds of worries better than a good focus on the setting being strong.

For example, say you have a customer who doesn't understand why a diamond ring costs so much. You can point out that the materials that go into jewelry have a major impact on its cost. Eighteen-karat gold is more expensive than fourteen-karat gold because there's more gold in the alloy. Another prime consideration is the amount of individual work that's involved in making the piece. Nowadays, most jewelry is mass-produced. However, that's not necessarily a negative. Mass production requires creativity, expertise, and effort. But the expense of these things is spread over a large number of items, reducing the cost of each unit. In contrast, while custom-designed jewelry offers uniqueness, each piece must bear the entire cost of the process. So, custom-made jewelry is always more expensive than comparable mass-produced items.

Use your product knowledge as a base of every sale that you make. Customers do not know about the fascinating world of jewelry. Guide them through the fantastic history of the piece that they are purchasing. It will create the same wonder in their soul as our ancestors did when they first believed that diamonds were the teardrops of the Gods. They will be begging to take something home and will take your opinions more seriously because they acknowledge that you are the expert.

Always expand your product knowledge. Make it a goal every day to learn something new about this fascinating world that you get to be a part of. Use a couple of minutes of your downtime to do some research, it doesn't take much time. I guarantee that it will be for your benefit. You want to always be prepared, don't you?

CHAPTER 6: GREET AND CONNECT

Too often we underestimate the power of a touch, a smile, a kind word, a listening ear, an honest compliment, or the smallest act of caring, all of which have the potential to turn a life around.
Leo Buscaglia

You only get one shot at a first impression, so make it count. When walking into a new environment, the human instinct is to automatically scan for threats. Jewelry stores are scary, especially to men. Jewelry stores are symbols of commitment, and not just any commitment, they are committing to being with someone for the rest of their life. It has taken a lot of courage to get them to your door. Now, it is your responsibility to welcome your customers the same way you would an old friend.

The customer will unknowingly form an opinion about you in the first few moments of entering your store. If that opinion is negative your chances of success are instantly diminished. If that opinion is positive, then you have already built the groundwork for them to trust your knowledge and skills. Positive first impressions are key to beginning any interaction you will have with a customer.

You need to stand out above the rest. This is not your everyday purchase. What they are buying is an expression of commitment, of passion and all the goopy love things you can imagine.

It has been said that you have three seconds to make a first impression. Customers will begin forming an opinion of you before a single word ever starts to form on your lips, which means appearance is everything!

Step one: you must be presentable long before you go to work. Get haircuts regularly, brush your teeth, polish your shoes, put on your desired amount of make-up and above all else wear deodorant. Your customers are genuinely scared, and when people are scared all their senses are heightened, including their sense of smell. Don't let them think they made the wrong decision with you. Keep a spare stick of deodorant at work along with something to keep your breath smelling fresh (but never ever chew gum in front of a customer. Use a stick to refresh your breath and then spit it out before a customer walks in).

When it comes to how to dress, ask yourself this question. "What do people think a jeweler should look like?". Well, what is a jeweler? The name itself originates from the old French word "joel" meaning jewel. From this we deduce that a jeweler sells jewels which are high valued items that are incredibly rare in nature. A jeweler then will take care that his/her appearance does not take away from the experience of their customers. A jeweler should dress so that they add to the customer experience. With this in mind, dress how you deem appropriate to add to the experiences of your customers.

You need to be in your best threads, dressed to the nines, hair perfectly coiffed. It doesn't matter if the place you are working has a casual dress code. You need to dress up because this is the first step of the most important moments of your customer's life.

A jeweler will also be proud of what they are selling. If you genuinely appreciate the value that comes from owning high quality jewelry, then you will wear it. Customers can sense the hypocrisy of you trying to sell them on why jewelry is so amazing if you yourself do not own any.

If you wear it, you will sell it.

Now, this does not mean that you should go out and buy yourself a juicy 3 carat diamond necklace. Instead, invest in some jewelry pieces for yourself that will add to your working wardrobe. For men, the first thing you should do is get a watch from a brand you sell. It will build your confidence in the brand, allow you to show how well they take everyday scruffs and keep you on time. For women there are a lot more options. It is recommended to start with a necklace that your store carries that is plain, simple, and can go with every outfit. It will amaze you the number of times you are going to be able to sell what you are wearing. Humans are visual creatures and when they see how good something looks on you, they will want it for themselves. If a partner is purchasing a gift for another, seeing it worn on another human being is validation that that product is a good one because it is what another human being likes.

Once you have trimmed your beard or curled your hair, applied deodorant and dressed appropriately you are ready to greet your customers. The first couple moments when a customer walks into your store you should greet them with a genuine smile and making direct eye contact. This immediately sends out positive signals and messages. You are someone to be trusted. You love your job and you are excited to help them. Most importantly, it lets the customer know that you like them.

Most men who walk into a store are completely out of their element. Do they want to be in a jewelry store? No. Do they want to spend all their hard-earned money? No. What will they most likely respond when you ask, "How can I help you?". They will say, "No thanks, I am just browsing."

Selling is about getting a string of yes's that will turn into your customer saying yes to a big sale. You never want to start off with a no. Starting off with a no puts your customer on the defense and shifts their mind into a state of declinement. Meaning that they will say "No" long before they say yes simply because that is how their state of mind has shifted. This 'no' attitude can kill a sale before you ever start pulling pieces out of cases.

You also don't want to dive into right into a sales presentation. Take a deep breath and take your time. Customers can be sensitive to the dynamics of the situation. Make them feel at home, make them feel like you care about them personally. They are more than just a sale. They are human beings full of emotions. Most sales associates forget this, but once you can recognize that each customer is bringing you a unique opportunity to help them express their desires that is when you will have a lifetime customer.

Customers can sense when you aren't being genuine. So, in order to give them a genuine smile you need to be excited to see them. You can be excited for a lot of different reasons. You can be excited that this is your chance to be able to hear someone's love story. Maybe this is your chance to practice all the skills you learned from reading Adornment. You can even focus on how this is your opportunity to make a new sale. It doesn't matter why you are genuinely smiling you simply need to find your reason.

Now that you have given them your best smile, it is time to open your mouth. If the first thing that a customer hears when they walk in is, "How can I help you?" I will throat punch you.

Don't ever ever EVER EVER start off that way. If this is how you approach every customer than you are shooting yourself in the foot. Don't ever Ever EVER EVER start off that way. Am I making this clear?

I do not want a nod, I want a "yes sir".
I am not kidding, I want you to say, "yes sir".
....

Good, now you can make some money.

The reason for my animosity towards this silly phrase is rooted deeply in the retail world. I just googled 'why we should never start with "how can i help you"' and these were all on the first page.

• The Absolute Worst Question To Ask: How Can I Help You? - Forbes

• 17 Things You Should Never Say if You Want to Be Taken Seriously ...

• 5 Phrases You Should Never Use In An Email - Fast Company

• 13 Things You Should Never Say At Work - Forbes

• Things to Never Say in an Interview - The Muse

"How can I help you" should be dropped from your vocabulary.

Unlearn it.
Forget it.
Move on.
And for your own happiness don't give it a second thought.

I am so passionate about dropping this sentence because you hear it at every retail store you walk into. You are already trained to say automatically reply by saying no. There is another reason why I want you to drop it. You hear it at every retail store.

You are asked "How can I help you" when you are at Home Depot picking out toilet seats, when you are at the grocery store looking at meats, when you walk into car shops and everywhere else that is a mundane part of everyday life.

You are more than that. You are selling some of the most priceless items on the market.

Try to think of all the things you immediately hear when you walk into those stores and avoid using them. Phrases like: May I help you, how are you, what brings you in today just to name a few. These phrases invite them to respond as they have always responded.
"I am just looking." or they brush you off entirely.

If you sound like everyone else, they treat you like everyone else. If you want to end a conversation with a customer, just ask if you can help. They are getting something special for their special someone so treat them as such. Set yourself apart. Greeting and connecting with your customer is the single most crucial step in the sales process. Some might even argue that your job is ultimately connecting with customers. You can't do that if you allow them to brush you off. One of the most successful ways to avoid these brush-offs is to start off by giving a compliment.

Give a Compliment.

This is the easiest way to welcome a customer into your store, but you have to be careful. If you do it wrong, you be construed as being a phony and will lose the most important thing you need to sell — trust. So, don't offer a general complement such as, "Don't you look good today" because it is disingenuous and kind of creepy. Instead make sure your compliment is relevant and specific. Try something along the lines of,

"That scarf is terrific",

"I see you are a Packers fan. I am too!".

Find something that you can genuinely compliment your customer for. If you find that there is nothing you can naturally compliment on, then don't. There are plenty of other ways to greet your customer, so don't worry about coming off as a phony.

After you have given your compliment it is important to start a conversation.

"That scarf is terrific, where did you get it?"

"I see that you are a Packers fan, I am too! Did you see their game last night?"

Jewelry is an especially good thing to compliment. You are a jeweler, so you naturally have an eye for quality pieces. Complimenting said jewelry is understanding that every jewelry piece carries a lot of emotional attachment. If you compliment someone on a previous purchase, then they will feel good about making that choice. It may help put them in the moment where they were proposed to or remind them of their grandmother who gave it to them. With some luck they may even tell you the story behind it and open themselves up for finding common ground and building rapport.

Opened Ended Questions

If there isn't something about that immediately catches your eye to compliment, you should ask an open-ended question:

"Are you enjoying your afternoon?"

"How'd you hear about us?"

"Did you watch the game last night? I stayed up late to watch the end!"

Ask them something to get the conversation flowing and doesn't catch them off guard. Try to avoid any yes or no questions because there is a 50% chance they will say no, and that is ultimately what you are trying to avoid.

The one yes and no question that can come out when you are first greeting your walk-in is this; ask if the customer has ever visited the store. There have been studies done that by asking if a customer had frequented an establishment before increased retail sales some 16 percent. The reasoning behind this is that when a customer audibly acknowledges they have used your services before it reminds them that they've been at your business before, so it's a familiar place. Familiarity means trust. And if there is trust, there is a willingness to spend money.

There are right and wrong ways to ask the questions, we are only going to go over the right ways. "Is this your first time visiting with us?" With visit it's more comfortable. You want to avoid the implication that this is a pressured sales environment. A fun way to remember to use visits is to think about how you meet people. Friends visit. Family stops by. Strangers come in or are brought in. Remember, you want these customers to be your friends, so use visits.

After you have established that they are indeed a first-time customer then it is time to start building your rapport and reputation. "May I ask who told you about us?" That question implies that your store values referral business and gets a lot of it.

However, some customers are so trained that no matter the question you ask they will respond with a "I am just looking". While this is not the beginning step, we were hoping for do not let this shut you down. So, what does it mean when a prospect says, "I'm just looking…"?

- The prospect has the purchase of something in mind
- The prospect may not yet have an idea of how much they will spend or can afford
- The prospect may not have a clear idea of when they would make a purchase or if they can

Do this:
"My best customers do the same thing. My name's Grant, and yours?"

"Excellent, we have a great selection of products to choose from, what are you most interested in looking at?"

"Of course. I understand. I want to assist you in any way I can. May I ask you a few quick questions so that I can help as much as possible in your search?"

Merchandise Greeting

Say that you are currently browsing through your inventory better familiarizing yourself with what treasures your store holds when a customer walks in. This is a great opportunity to start off your interaction by simply holding up whatever piece you are holding and say,

"Hello there. I was just looking at one of our newest pieces, do you want to see it? It has the deepest shade of blue"

"Hello there, you came in at just the right time, we just received this new piece in and I was hoping to get someone's opinion on it?"

Using merchandise to spark a customer's curiosity is a great way to break down walls while simultaneously showing a piece that a customer may not have had in mind but will fall in love with. It acts as both a conversation started and will lead to more sales down the line.

Service Greeting

Now that you have tried a couple of different openers it is time to really show your customers what a caring jeweler you are. You are going to do something special for your customer for absolutely nothing in return. You are going to offer them a service.

"Hello there! Did you come in today for a free ring cleaning?"

"Would you like me to polish your jewelry for free while you look around? It will only take a moment."

Be sure to mention that the service is free and quick. Otherwise, how will they know that it is free and quick? Most people walking into your store have not had their jewelry polished their entire lives. They have no idea what it takes to polish something and instead of asking you if its free and feeling like they are being cheap they will just say no. People are terrified of looking like idiots and the best way of protecting themselves is to refuse and say no. However, when you present them with more information you are giving them just what they need to be able to trust you with their priceless jewelry.

Again, it is important to remember that most people

have never had their jewelry polished in their entire life. This means that their rings, watches, earrings, bracelets and necklaces have been roughed up a little. You have the chance to rejuvenate their iridescence. If you can successfully clean their jewelry to the point where it looks like new you transport them back in time. Because you cleaned their jewelry so well you aren't just handing them back diamonds and gold, you are giving them a chance to look back on memories. Their eyes light up and a huge smile come across their face as they proclaim that it hasn't looked this good since the day they received it. Reminding them of that day sparks up old emotions and reminds them of one of two things.

1. What if felt like to give that gift and fully express how you feel
2. The love and gratitude they had when they were given that gift

These old motions will set the tone for gift giving and gift receiving for the rest of the time that those customers are in your store. They will want to feel those emotions again and the conduit for expressing and receiving those emotions happens to be right in front of them resting softly behind locked glass. You are priming the selling well for a successful close.

Along with preparing yourself for a successful sale, giving service right off the bat sets a high bar for the standard of care that they are going to receive at your store. Not only that, but even if you don't close the sale that day then the next jeweler they go to who asks if they can clean their jewelry will get a "no thanks, I just had it cleaned at another jeweler." Trust me, it is an unexpected slap in the face to some sales associates. Even veteran salesman can be thrown off their rhythm because they aren't used to getting shot down from giving free jewelry cleanings. This could give you an unseen edge because that moment of fluster may steer that customer away from them and back towards you.

Show People Around

A salesperson should show first-time customers around the store and add some personal touches. The salesperson could say, for example, "That's my favorite area of the store—that's where the diamonds are."

Find Common Ground

Once you have broken the ice you are in total control of the conversation. You can restrict and regulate the speed, tone, and seriousness of what you are talking about. You have the helm and can steer it any which way, so use it to your advantage. Set yourself apart during your icebreaker and show your customer that you are going to give them top notch service.

Set yourself apart right at the kickoff by giving the customer your undivided attention. Even if you are in the middle of doing paperwork, cleaning the glass or doing some other task you need to stop what you are doing once they walk through your door.

Never allow your customer to feel like they are a hindrance. You can always finish paperwork or clean up your mess later, but you can only make one first impression. You need to let them know that they are more important than your everyday tasks.

If someone walks in while you are with a customer already, let them know that you still care about them by diverting your attention away from your current clients just long enough to give them a quick smile and let them know that someone will be with them shortly.

Once you have greeted your customer begin to find common ground as soon as possible. Remember the next two things I am about to tell you.

1) People like people who like the things they like.
2) People buy from people they like

Finding common ground is surprisingly easy but takes genuine effort. You have to give genuine answers and genuinely care about what the other person has to say. Let's consider that someone has just walked into your store and you have the following conversation:

Jeweler: "Hello there, sir! How's the weather outside?"
Customer: "Very cold."

So, what can we discern so far? We know that your customer is in your store and you are going to close him today. We also know that it is cold outside. Although it doesn't seem like much, this is all the information you need to start your connection process with your customer. To do so, all you need to do is to start asking questions to get to know them.

Jeweler: "Are you a cold weather person?"
Customer: "I love the heat, can't stand the winter."

Woohoo! You learned your first bit of information about this customer. He has unknowingly given you an opportunity to find common ground.

Jeweler: "Me too. I am originally from California, so I am not used to the cold yet. Nothing beats the warm sunshine on your face, am I right?"

Finding common ground is as easy as that. All you have to do is ask your customer questions to get to know them. However, sometimes your interests won't align. You can't connect if you aren't being honest. Customers can tell when you are being dishonest because they can taste your lies. However, just because you don't share common interests doesn't mean you can't find common ground. Let's look at this scenario again, but instead of you being a fan of summer you are more of a winter lover.

Jeweler: "Are you a cold weather person?"

Customer: "I love the heat, can't stand the winter."

Jeweler: "Ah yes, the heat is when you can go to the beach and is the best time of year to enjoy fresh lemonade. Do you have any fun plans for this upcoming summer?"

Notice that the jeweler didn't just come out and say, "I am more of a winter person myself" even though that is a completely honest response. Instead jewelers should choose to build common ground by saying a couple of the elements that they honestly enjoy about summer. You can use this tactic with just about anything. Your customer is going on their third cruise, but you have never stepped foot on a ship?

"That must be so fun, I have always wanted to go on cool adventures like that. Where are you going? The Caribbean sounds like a blast. Is your trip what brings you in today?"

Overall, the biggest thing you need to remember when welcoming a customer into your store is this. Welcome customers as if they're friends coming to your house. That means welcoming them with a big smile, eye contact, and lots of enthusiasm. When your best friend comes into the store, you are going to be enthusiastic. You are going to want to connect with them and have a good time. They are here to celebrate special occasions and you get to be a part of it, so get excited.

Overcoming I am Just Looking

Sometimes, no matter how well you greet and connect they will say "No thanks, I am just looking." If you put your best foot forward and attempted to become their lifetime jeweler, then it's okay. Don't be offended or think you have done something wrong. For many, the - I am just looking - phrase is a defense mechanism that automatically springs once they are greeted regardless of your genuine compliments or open-ended questions.

There are two things to keep in mind whenever you hear a "I am just looking"

1. They are liars. You don't go to a car dealership if there isn't some desire in you to purchase a car.

2. Nothing is more satisfying than someone closing someone who said they were just looking.

Entice them. Inspire them. Fuel Their passion. You got this.

The first thing you should do is to remember that they are here for a purpose and without help they will not get what they are after. So, if you get told, "I am just looking" the first thing you should do is help them find whatever they are looking for. For example, you could say,

"That sounds like fun, is there anything you need help finding?"

Nine times out of ten, that is all they need before they begin breaking down their walls and telling you what it is they are really after. From there, you can ask questions like who it is for and what the occasion is, but we will get more into that later in our questions chapter.

If your first attempt doesn't work, then you give them a quick verbal map of the layout of your store. Don't go into detail describing every nook and cranny, just give them a quick couple of sentences letting them know where your rings, necklaces, and bracelets are and then back off.

As you give them a verbal map, customers will either

come clean and tell you what they are really looking for, or they will almost immediately start going in the direction of where they want to be. Once you know what section they are drawn to, give them a minute to get a quick glance over and then do one of these options:

1.   Tell them that you just got a new piece (that is conveniently in the same case that they are looking at) and you were wondering if they could give their opinion.

2.   Ask you customer if they would like to try on something from the case.

Option #1 works great because you are no longer making it about you, you are now asking for a favor. People love to give favors, especially when it comes down to being something that they may or may not like for themselves. Most importantly, you are taking away the chance for them to tell you no. You aren't asking if you can show them something, you are telling them to give their opinion on a new piece of jewelry.

Option #2 is much weaker and is much easier to get a "no" as an answer. If confidence is hard to come by, this is a great way to build up your courage to getting to option #1. However, you should wean yourself off of this as soon as possible. The reason for that is because once your customer has said no to you twice, you are done. It is time to have another sales associate come in and finish. If you don't then you are just pestering them at that point.

CHAPTER 7: BUILDING RAPPORT

I've learned that people will forget what you said, people will forget what you did, but people will never forget how you made them feel.
Maya Angelou

Past personal experiences or the stories of families and friends have made people very wary of those who are selling anything. This book contains more information about diamonds than the average person knows without doing extensive and exhausting research. Most of your customers will not look up anything beyond comparing prices on the internet. This unfamiliarity with the true value of diamonds can add a lot of pressure because they fear that they are going to get ripped off.

Combine this with the fact that this wariness increases with the monetary value along with the emotional weight of the purchase and you've got an overwhelmed and anxious customer. It is no wonder that most people who walk into a jewelry store are expecting to be ambushed.

The best way to combat this fear is to build rapport with your customer. If you don't know what rapport is I have looked up the definition for you. According to

Webster, rapport is a friendly, harmonious relationship. My trainer explained it to me as getting to know your customers on a more personal level.

Building rapport usually begins after you greet your customer. You have already made eye-contact, smiled, and given your non-business greeting. Conversation will usually flow naturally into small chitchat. From there you need to look for areas of common ground or interest that you sincerely care about. People can tell when you are being phony.

You might make a comment or ask a question about local events, seasonal activities, sports, weather – even traffic. Since most people like to talk about themselves, you can often use that to get the conversation rolling. The presence of children is another natural starting point (But never guess about the age or gender of a baby. Saying that their little boy is adorable when it is a girl can upset some customers).

If you ever wonder what to not talk about try to treat every conversation like it is happening at a Thanksgiving dinner party. Avoid talking about politics, religion and any subjects that may be deemed too personal. Never ask when someone is "due" to have their baby. It will end poorly one in every four times and you will probably never see that person again.

Once you have completed your non-business greeting feel free to introduce yourself whenever you feel it fits but try to get your name in sooner rather than later. Usually, after introducing yourself your customer will respond by saying their name. If they don't, it is okay to ask what it is. A good rule of thumb is to always try to introduce yourself early on. How can you have a 20-minute conversation with someone if you don't know their name?

Learning each other's names is the first step to building your rapport and eventually making a sale. Pay close attention to how they prefer to be addressed. Most will go by their first name such as Ashlee or Jason. However, on occasion they might say that their name is Mr. Jones. Respect that they wish to be addressed as Mr. Jones and refer to your customer as such as you go throughout your presentation.

Once you hear their name, use it. Names are more powerful than you realize. They add depth to your conversation and help your rapport grow faster than just saying you. Let me give you an example.

Average Salesman: "What do you think your girlfriend will do when she sees you on one knee with this ring?"

Jeweler: "Jason, what do you think Ashlee will do when she sees you on one knee with this ring?"

Occasionally I have had trainees who struggled remembering their customer's names after introductions. This is a common occurrence and it can be improved quite easily. The first step to remembering a customer's name is the simplest. Actively try to remember it.

Don't be lazy during introductions and simply brush off their name the same as you have done in everyday conversations. By simply attempting to focus and actively trying to remember their name you will instantly be more successful at recalling names. You may have heard that by looking at a person's nose while saying their name helps you recall it later on. I believe that the reason this works is because you are first actively attempting to remember their name. You can stare at noses all day long and not remember a single name. You have to care about remembering their name.

Once you care enough to pay attention to their name you will remember their name the more you use it. Periodically throw their name in by asking your customer questions about their future spouse or where they work. Hearing their name from you will reinforce that you care about them, build the rapport you are looking for and eventually help you close the sale. There is a point where you can overuse a person's name, but you are a human being and can tell when too much is too much.

Ask questions that will have your customers open up. Open ended questions - questions that cannot be answered with a yes or no - are fantastic for breaking down walls and move towards making a sale. Good salesman asks how long a couple has been together, what occasion brings them into the store and which anniversary they are celebrating. A jeweler will say…

"Describe how…

"I'd really like to know ..

"I'd like to hear some of the ideas you've been kicking around".

The more you know the better you will sell.

For instance, say you know that a young man named Dakota has come into your store to buy an engagement ring. They have been dating for 9 months and are hoping to get married in September which is 5 months away. He is a student and is going to graduate in a year and a half.

With this information you can tell him how we are giving him a free lifetime diamond warranty, so he never has to worry about losing his diamonds. Maybe you can tell him about your other warranties and press him to make the purchase so that they can start planning their wedding right away. But that isn't enough information. You are asking good questions, but it isn't building enough rapport. Good rapport digs a little deeper.

A jeweler would find out that Dakota has been dating Katilyn for 9 months. Kaitlyn is left-handed and wants to get married in September because that is when her parents got married. Dakota is studying Economics and will graduate in a year and a half. After he graduates, he wants to move to South Carolina to be closer to family.

This information is almost the same as we had before, but because we got to know Dakota personally, we got to know him beyond the usual get to know you questions. Now we can add value to all our services. A Jeweler would say,

"Dakota, since you and Kaitlyn are going to be together forever you are going to want a ring that can last forever. We are even giving you a free lifetime diamond warranty to go with it. That will be great because Kaitlyn is left-handed and left-handed people use their wedding ring hand more often and it bumps into more things. These extra bumps put a little more wear and tear on her ring, but she won't have to worry about it because Kaitlyn will be protected with that diamond warranty.

"Because you are an Economics man, you understand the value of good service. Here at [my store] we have a service plan that covers all the work the goldsmith will put unto it so you never have to spend another dollar on this ring. Imagine having a car that you never needed to pay oil changes, tire rotations, or any of that regular maintenance on. This service plan is exactly like that and will save you hundreds of dollars while giving you peace of mind knowing that you are protected.

"You'll be happy to know that we are nationwide, so those service plans and diamond warranty cover you no matter where you move. We have a store just 20 minutes away from where you are moving. You won't have to mail Kaitlyn's ring anywhere so there is no chance of it getting lost in the mail. We will be able to take care of you. No matter where you go."

The more you learn, the better prepared you'll be to make suggestions. Use their names and you will remember them. People love hearing their name and it makes them feel special. Throughout introductions and building rapport you learn information that will add tremendous value to your store and help you stand out above the rest of the competition. However, a customer should not feel that they are being interrogated with your questions.

Let conversation flow naturally and ask relative questions as they occur. You shouldn't just blab all your expertise on them at once. Give it to them piece by piece. They will not remember what you said, but they will feel the value that you bring to the table throughout their entire visit. When they leave your doors, they will know that you have the best value in your town regardless of price.

Also be careful to avoid questions the customer might have to answer with, "I don't know." Rather than "What's his favorite color?" you might try "Name a few colors you think he looks good in."

As you learn about your customer you must keep the tone positive. It is not enough to simply learn about a potential client, you must be engaged. If you make a compliment, be sincere about it. If you are not genuinely interested in the questions you ask or the answers you receive than you are going to be seen as a fake. No one wants to have someone pretend that they care about your identity. Humans crave genuine concern and friendship. Here are some tips on how you can approach your customer with more sincerity:

1)   Use Sincere Body Language.

Body language can convey a great deal about your attitude, and it can easily reveal sincerity (or a lack thereof). When you interact with others, try to be mindful of your posture, mannerisms, and behavior.

One of the biggest things you can do is to make steady eye contact, but don't stare. Look away every now and then, and don't forget to blink. While you talk, maintain a relaxed posture, but keep your body slightly poised. You can do this by very slightly leaning toward the person you're talking to or reaching out/gesturing towards that person. Don't try to overly change your body language to reflect sincerity. If you're sincere, your body language will naturally show it.

2)   Be an Active Listener.

One easy way to show sincerity to others is by being an active listener. As someone speaks to you, keep an open mind about what that person is saying. Practicing active listening skills show others that you are taking a sincere interest in what they have to say, and that you genuinely want to know more about the thoughts and feelings of others.

Face the person you're talking to. When you have a genuine reaction to what someone else is saying, your facial cues will give that reaction away. Your eyebrows will raise, your eyes may widen, and your mouth will reveal your emotional reaction. Facing someone will let them see your reactions, and it will convey to them that you are engaged and interested.

Ask open-ended questions to allow the other person to elaborate. For example, don't just ask, "Did you like living there?" This type of question will elicit a yes or no response. Instead, you can ask something like, "Wow, I've never been there before. What was it like for you? What are some memories you have of living there?" This shows your engagement and your curiosity.

A secret to good conversation is to often pause and reflect on what has been said by the other person before giving your own response. Your conversational partner may be thinking of how to phrase something, or simply leaving a pause in the conversation for dramatic effect. If you rush to say whatever is on your mind, it will not convey a sincere conversational interest in that person's thoughts and opinions.

3)   Understand Another's Point of View.
If you refuse to consider why another person thinks/feels the way they do, you will not be able to have a sincere conversation with that person. Understanding someone else's point of view does not necessarily mean abandoning your own perspective. Rather, you should try to understand what motivates others, and what life experiences may have shaped another person's point of view. Once you are capable of seeing the world through someone else's eyes, you'll develop a more sincere understanding of who that person is and what made him the way he is.

Instead of criticizing someone else's musical tastes, for example, try to understand what about that music might be appealing. Perhaps the lyrics speak to the other person. Or perhaps the loud bass lines of a dance song allow someone who is normally shy to break out of her shell and make moves on the dance floor.

Before you argue with someone about politics, try to understand why that person holds his or her values. Someone who was raised by immigrants who grew up very poor might have strong opinions about the experience of immigrants, which could affect that person's political ideology. Seeing the world through someone else's perspective helps you become less judgmental and more compassionate.

God gave us two ears and one mouth, and the amount of talking to listening should be the same ratio. No customer wants to know how you got engaged 12 years ago (unless you feel that you are deep enough in your rapport that they trust you as their liaison of decision making). Listen actively to the customer's statements and responses. Let the customer know you're paying attention by maintaining eye contact, nodding, and smiling in agreement at appropriate points. Keep the revelations coming by injecting an occasional "Oh?", "How so?", "I see," "That's interesting," or "Tell me more."

Show them that you respect what they have to say by following the golden rule of listening. Never interrupt your customer. The customer can interrupt you because them interrupting is their immediate reaction to what you are explaining/telling. They are excited or curious or swallowed up in whatever you are telling them. Use that to your advantage.

The more you learn, the better prepared you'll be to make suggestions.

Whenever I have trained new jewelers to the idea of building rapport, I have always tried to have this be the foundation that they build on. What makes this person unique? Each person who walks into your store has spent a lifetime dodging sales folk trying to get them to purchase the newest and greatest gadget for 20% off. However, they chose to come to you because they need your help. They don't know anything about jewelry or carats or the benefits of buying from a brick and mortar store. You need to be there for them as a friend. Get to know them as you present your jewelry pieces. It will not only build a lasting relationship, but it will allow you to better tailor your sales presentation. When you know someone and the plans that they have you can connect benefits and features on a personal level. Do that, and you will sell them on anything. You want to be able to sell any customer anything, don't you?

CHAPTER 8: TOOLS AND SHOWING

Believe you can and you're halfway there.
Theodore Roosevelt

Being a jeweler means that you are in showbusiness. Much like a magician or a singer, you must know how to use the tools of the trade. How you handle the pieces you sell can enhance its allure and add to its value. A good magician will never reveal his tricks, but we're jewelers so sharing secrets is totally fine.

Tools that should be in the hands of every jeweler are polishing cloths, counter pads, ring sticks and mirrors. If your store sells loose diamonds, you will also have diamond papers, tweezers, and one or more diamond holders. While these tools may seem simple in function and design, they're one of the best ways to build value and close sales. For that reason, it's important to know how to use them effectively.

Polishing Cloths
When you present jewelry pieces you want them to look their very best. The second that a piece leaves the case it should immediately be polished using the cloth. Do

not immediately hand jewelry to a customer without it getting that polish. This little added effort will erase any smudges or fingerprints from showings of old. Imagine trying to buy a car and when you look inside there are old McDonalds bags lying on the floor. It will be an immediate turn off.

When you gently caress a piece of jewelry, you are not just cleaning it. You are subtly showing a customer that jewelry is a precious, worthwhile thing. It has immense beauty and value and should be cared for accordingly. This subconscious reaction will help you in your quest to build value. Polish every piece.

The polishing is also a good time for you to hide the ace up your sleeve during your magic show. Use this time to look at the tag. Notice the price, carat weight, any other notable features and quickly memorize them. By doing this, you look like a true expert by answering any of their questions like you knew that piece by heart.

Counter Pads

Counter pads are underutilized and poorly named. They should be used in every presentation. Counter pads are the stage where you get to present piece by piece in wonderful spotlight. If I had my way, I would rename them stages. It portrays their use much better than just pads that sit on the counter.

By placing the stage on the counter in an elegant, gentle manner is a great way to show your professionalism. You understand its importance and it sets the stage for your presentations. Place the pad directly in front of your customer. If there is a ring slot turn it towards the customer so that they don't have to bend over the case to inspect their choices. Along with being a stage for you to guide your show, it also narrows the focus of the customer to a single piece. If you do not use the stage, there is a chance that your customer will get distracted by all the shiny alternatives below instead of the piece you have handpicked for them.

You will get better reactions from your customers because of the forced focus to the stage. If they immediately go from the piece you have spotlighted back to the case, then you can tell that they do not see it as the piece for them. But when you find one that really catches their attention it will be very apparent because they will forget everything else that your store has to offer.

The stage also serves as a great cushion in case of any accidents. Nobody is perfect and on occasion you are going to drop something. The stage will make a dangerous fall end in a cushy landing. When a piece hits the floor or smacks onto the counter it can create a distraction from your performance. Keep the focus on them and the life choices that they are making.

These stages reflect the professionalism of you and your entire store. There will be some wear and tear with time. Don't let your all your hard work be thrown out by using shabby stages. If Taylor Swift wouldn't perform on it, replace it.

Ring Sticks
Sometimes referred to as fingers, ring sticks are cylindrical rods specifically used to show rings. Unlike the other tools we have already discussed, these are not used in every presentation. Ring sticks are used to help your clients visualize how pieces will look like on a finger.

It is always much more beneficial for a customer to try on and handle the ring for themselves. Physical involvement is key to sales. The ring stick is a substitute for when that cannot happen. If the ring is too small to fit on a client's finger it is much more beneficial for them to see it on the ring stick than it is to try it on a different finger on a different hand.

The ring stick is also useful for when a man is shopping for a woman or vice versa. Men will almost always feel more comfortable handling a ring on a ring stick than just holding the ring itself. There is a sense of security knowing that it won't slip between their fingers as they inspect it from every angle. The same goes for women shopping for men.

It is also beneficial to model the ring for them. Men and women are incredibly visual. The more realistic it can become in their head the more likely you are to make a sale. Once a man is able to narrow his choices down to just a couple rings, offer to have one of your female associates model it for him. Same goes for a woman shopping for a man. This modeling helps them see what a ring will look like on a real person. Your associate can then reinforce what you have told the customer and help you close the sale.

Mirrors

The question that every person is wondering in the back of their head during a jewelry purchase is how it will look when they wear it. Seeing themselves wear the piece in the mirror not only lets them know what it looks like on them, it also creates physical involvement. You can create the mental and emotional involvement as you build rapport. This kind of multi-level involvement is what you should strive for in every encounter with a customer.

Women command up to 60% of all disposable income. Help them feel beautiful about themselves and celebrate their successes. Strategically place mirrors throughout your store ranging from countertop mirrors to larger mirrors that let customers gage how they look from across the room.

As with all the tools, be sure to keep them clean. Professionals do not allow their mirrors to get dirty.

Diamond Papers

These envelope-like papers are used to separate diamonds from each other. With each diamond carefully folded in diamond paper they add organization, cleanliness and safety to diamond presentations.

When you present a diamond wrapped warmly in its envelope you must be careful. Inside is a loose diamond so unwanted movements can cause the diamond to fling across the room. As a jeweler you want to only open diamond papers above your counter pad. You also want to avoid touching the inside of the diamond paper so that the diamond doesn't get exposed to too many oils.

Once you have uncovered the diamond treat it as you would any other jewelry piece and polish it with a polishing cloth specifically used for diamonds only. From there, take the diamond paper and place it somewhere the customer will not get distracted by any of the specifications and remained enamored by the diamond you have unveiled.

Glass

Easily the most underappreciated tools at a jeweler's disposal. The glass is your customer's portal to the world of artfully crafted precious metals and gems. Through the glass an entirely new world is available to them. Would you want that gateway to the diamond world to be blurry and smudged? Of course not.

People will judge you the second they walk through your door. They are expecting to work with a professional and that is why you must look professional, smell professional, act like a professional and be in a professional environment. Smudges on your glass make you look unprofessional, uncaring and frankly sluggish. If you were spending thousands of dollars and your salesman was any of those three things, how do you think you would feel? Clean the glass immediately after each customer gets a presentation but wait until they have left your store. Nobody wants to feel like they made a mess.

If you haven't noticed, there has been an underlying theme here. Keep things clean. Keep things neat and in order. Look presentable. Smell presentable. Be an entertainer. Razzle and dazzle everyone who was ever curious about diamonds. Don't let yourself fall into laziness. Be the professional that your prospects are expecting out of a jeweler.

Inventory Assortment

Now that you know what tools you have at your disposal it is time to move on to what you have in stock. That's right, this is where you get to start digging into your inventory. Knowing what you have available, how much items costs and where particular pieces are located is going to help you make better suggestions for your customer. If you have a customer looking for opals and you don't know where they are imagine A) how embarrassing that would be B) how much less your customer is going to trust you and what you say you can't even find the opals. If you can't even find them, why should I believe that you know so much about them?

You need to know where specific items are in specific price ranges. You will look more professional and your customers will be more confident in your knowledge and recommendations. In order to know your inventory, you must do more than look at it through the glass. Go through and touch each piece. Inspect every item and look at them in detail. Find pieces that will match, colors that coordinate well and potential add on items. You can use these combos later to increase your items per ticket.

While you familiarize yourself, be sure to take note of some of your more favorite items. Choose a couple of items from each category of your inventory that stand out to you. You are more likely to sell an item if you like it and it allows you to make suggestions to customers without making any hesitations. Again, find a couple favorite pieces in each category. Use these are your go-to items.

If you have a store that is set up differently every day be sure that when you walk into work to immediately look around and see where everything is placed. It is hard to sell pieces when you don't know where they are.

When it comes to price you don't have to memorize the cost of each individual piece but be aware of what price category it falls under. Where are your most valuable solitaires? Where are your promise rings that are gold? What is the least expensive thing you sell? What is the price range for a 1 carat solitaire? Is anything on sale? Do you know where all your different styles are?

Put yourself in hypothetical situations where a customer asks for a certain style of jewelry, and then take them from the most expensive item you have in that category and work your way down to the smallest item. You will get very good at finding and showing all the styles you have to offer.

Knowing your inventory will help you solve your price, quality and style objections. For example, say a customer has fallen in love with a one carat diamond, but it puts them over budget. If you know that you have ¾ carat diamond that is the same quality as the one carat you will know to show it to them. You can put them in the price range that they can afford, and you will get the sale. Best case scenario, he doesn't like that it is smaller, and you can sell him on the benefit of owning a one carat diamond! It is a win-win no matter the situation as long as you know your customers options. Be in control by knowing.

You understand the tools that are at your disposal, you know where everything is and how certain pieces will look stunning together. To top it off you have grasped the art of the greet and connect and it is now time to start presenting your customer with actual jewelry. Yay!

Each presentation you give is going to have its own unique storyline to follow where you have to overcome unique objections. Because of these ever-shifting scenarios you need to become a master of basic showing techniques so that when each storm comes you will be able to navigate it with ease.

The very first thing you need to keep in your mind is the ABC's of selling:

A- Always
B- Be
C- Creating Value

It doesn't matter if you are selling necklaces, diamonds, or service plans. You should always be looking for ways to make what you are selling valuable in the eyes of your customers. You can add value in any number of ways. You can explain how rare gold is to show just how scarce this precious metal is and how lucky they are to get even a small bit of it. You may explain how your diamond warranty allows you to wear your jewelry every day without fear. Whatever comes out of your mouth should be building value in your company, your product and yourself.

Always be creating value. Always.

It is a mindset that you must get into, and it is something that you have to remind yourself of every day. Once the ABC's of selling are tattooed on the frontal cortex of your brain, you can begin focusing on the foundation of any sales presentation: features and benefits.

Features and Benefits
These are the basis upon which every sales presentation has been built upon since the dawn of selling itself. Once you understand how to present features and benefits you will not only sell more, but you are going to be more convincing in your everyday life. Let's begin by breaking it down.

Feature: A physical aspect of the jewelry
Benefit: How the feature makes your customers' lives better physically or emotionally.

Customers buy benefits. End of sentence. Period. They are buying what the item can do for them. For example, the Bugatti Veyron 16.4 supercar has 1,200 hp and a maximum torque of 1,500 Nm. Those two features are some of the most impressive on the market, but does it make it you want to buy it? Probably not. However, let's look at the benefit of having 1,200 hp and a maximum torque of 1,500 Nm. This raw power allows the Veyron to accelerate from 0 to 100 km/h in 2.5 seconds with a top speed of 415 km/h making it the fastest production supercar in the world. Can you hear the purr of its engines? Can you feel the wind become powerless as you speed on by in the fastest car the human race can create? That is the benefit of having 1,200 hp and a maximum torque of 1,500 Nm, and that is why people are going to buy it.

Naturally, you are going to want to highlight the features and benefits for your customer to show them the true value of what it is they are purchasing. Below are three different scenarios that can happen when using features and benefits.

Scenario 1: Feature then Benefit
"The cut on this diamond is rated as excellent. This means that it maximizes the light that goes into it and gives you the most brilliant diamond possible"

Scenario 2: Benefit, Feature then Feature
"This diamond maximizes the light that goes into it and gives you the most brilliance possible. The reason is because of the way that this diamond is cut. It is rated as excellent which is the highest rating possible "This is an H, SI1 one carat diamond. It's been certified by GIA. Its set in 18K white gold and its price is only $9700. Isn't it stunning?"

Scenario 3: Benefit, Feature, Benefit, Feature
"You have a great diamond here. You might even say that it is mesmerizing. That's because its cut to the highest standards in the industry. That's a great look, isn't it? (tie-down)"
"Yes, it is"
"And when you look at it closely it is flawless to the naked eye. So, when she shows her friends all they're going to see is how much her diamond sparkles. Do you know why?"
"Why?"
"It's because of the incredible quality of the......"

Looking at the three scenarios, choose the one that sweeps you off your feet by giving your customers the benefits of what you are giving them. Giving benefits and then explaining the reason behind it using "That's because" is going to close more sales for you. You are going to focus more on the benefits that the customer receives and sell more pieces because you are showing them the reason that it is awesome first before explaining why it's awesome.

Benefits are not benefits unless they are perceived as benefits to the customer. They have no idea what they need in a diamond. Not a clue. Sell your customers the benefits of having a ring that doesn't twirl on a finger because of its European shank or shines brighter because of its magnificent cut. Nobody will listen when you talk about a European shank. They may even block it out because it is boring. But they will NEVER forget about that ring that doesn't spin on their finger.

Using "that's because" when showing benefits and features is so powerful that Citibank decided to test the strength of the "that's because" statement by comparing two separate groups. In the first group, telemarketers called consumers and offered the Citi shopper service, telling them "Citi shopper can find you the lowest prices on over 200,000 name brand items." They explained the "consumer benefit" but failed to offer a plausible "reason why." Only a small percentage of consumers signed up.

In the second group they added a "that's because" statement. Here, the telemarketers said "Citi shopper can find you the lowest prices on over 200,000 name brand items. That's because our computers continually monitor prices at over 50,000 retailers nationwide, ensuring that you get the lowest price available anywhere."

With only that change in the script, enrollment skyrocketed. Why? Because Citibank told shoppers of the benefit -- finding the lowest prices nationwide -- then backed it up with a plausible reason why -- through their computers continually monitoring pricing at over 50,000 retailers nationwide. Use the "that's because" to educate and fascinate your customers so that they donate their time and money to you.

Cheap

Whenever you show jewelry you want to be building value. I want you to think of the last time you used the word cheap. Why did you use it? Was it to describe something valuable? No. Most likely it is because you were describing something as being really flimsy or unremarkable. Cheap is what you find at discount stores and used car lots. Nobody wants cheap products or services. What they want is a good value. Cheap suggests that the product is disposable or that it will quickly degrade and become useless in a short time. If you are in a hurry to downgrade the value of what you are selling a customer just say that ugly word.

Instead, when you are talking about how affordable your jewelry is use descriptive words that are more gentle, positive, and show that what you have to offer them has value.

Customer: "Where are your cheap necklaces?"

Jeweler: "You came to the right place. We have some of the most inexpensive diamond necklaces in the valley. What is the occasion?"

Get cheap out of your vocabulary. Get it our right now.

Creating Involvement

One of the best ways to establish value and create the

desire to own/give jewelry is by creating involvement. To do this you need to get the customer involved with every jewelry piece in three distinct ways –

1. Physically
2. Mentally
3. Emotionally

1. Physical – Physical involvement is one of the hidden treasures of selling jewelry. Buying jewelry is not a spectator sport. This is the part of the sales presentation where you let the customer hold, touch and try on pieces. When they are touching and feeling the jewelry their minds are focused on thinking about the jewelry. If they were just watching you present jewelry then you are letting their minds wander. When they are holding the jewelry in their hands, they aren't just thinking about what you are trying to sell them, they are experiencing it.

This power of experience is game changing. If your customer is purchasing something for themselves, one of the best things you can do is to ask if you can put the jewelry on your customer. Self-purchasing customers need to see how it looks on themselves. Instead of thinking that they would look cute, they can look in a mirror and know that they aren't just cute, they are royalty. One of the best things that you can do is to ask if you can put it on the customer. Handing them items across the counter is fine, but the experience is elevated when it is placed on them. They deserve that jewelry, and it is you that is bestowing that gift upon them.

It also provides you the rare opportunity to touch each other. It sounds super weird, I know, but it's a proven scientific fact that a simple physical touch is one of the fastest ways to build trust.

Let's not forget about our gift givers either. They too need to see what jewelry looks like on their significant other before they can make a purchase, but most likely that person will not be present. What do you do in that case? Do what Victoria's Secret did to sell billions of dollars in underwear. Get a model.

Request a co-worker to come over and try on the jewelry piece. If possible, try to match the gender of the person who will be wearing the jewelry. I.e. if a customer is looking for a watch for their boyfriend/husband/son ask a male associate to come and be your model. This allows the customer to use the least amount of imagination possible and truly see the piece in action. It also allows your customer to begin building the anticipation of being able to see it on their partner. Giving gifts is both a pleasurable experience and a stressful one. Make it as easy as possible by taking the guesswork out of it.

2. Mental – Mental involvement is a powerhouse hidden throughout the entire presentation. There is no one simple way to create mental involvement besides listening. Paying attention is going to be your best bet. That doesn't just mean that you listen to what they say. You are listening to the meaning behind their words. You are listening to their body language. You are listening to their needs and providing them with benefits that satisfy those needs.

When you listen you are showing that you care. When you care about what a customer truly wants then you can choose items that they will want to see. When you accomplish this, you can then translate the features into benefits for the customers unique position in life.

3. Emotional – Emotional involvement is what every customer really seeks when purchasing fine jewelry. The job of the jeweler then is to breath that emotion to life as you present. There is an old saying that goes, "Make a sell, you'll make a living. Sell a relationship and you can make a fortune."

The easiest way to get started in the emotional involvement is by using romance words like, "timeless", "captivating" "breathtaking". When they are handling touching and thinking about the piece you are presenting, they are becoming more and more emotionally involved. Keep reminding them of the meanings behind the reason you are giving jewelry. You are giving it to them because you love them, and they are going to love what you choose.

Showing Prices

Price is a very finicky thing. It can make people feel queasy if you say it in the wrong way. You don't want this finicky thing to disrupt your sales presentation, so you are going to leave it out of it. You read that right; I do not want you to bring up price until your customer brings it up. The first person to bring up price always loses.

Instead, try to focus on the design, color, and style of the pieces that you are showing them. It is also flattering if you show them the best that your store has to offer. There is a level of respect that people have for themselves, and by showing them high dollar items you are ultimately giving them that respect. You don't know their budget. They could be millionaires who popped by your shop for an afternoon stroll. Show them high and they will buy high because they will have fallen in love with the piece.

However, at some point in time you are going to have to talk about price. It is unavoidable. This next section is going to give you the run-down on the psychology of pricing so that you can use pricing to your advantage.

Psychology of Pricing

Say that you are going through and repricing the items in your store. Price changes are most effective when the far-left digit changes. A one-dollar difference between $789 and $790 won't matter. However, a one-dollar difference between $300 and $299 will make a huge difference.

Why is the left digit so important? Because your brain uses that first number as an anchor for the overall price.

What that means is that when a customer is in a room full of price tags his/her brain tries to keep things as simple as possible to avoid being overloaded. To keep things from overheating, the brain will lock onto the first number of a price tag and focus its attention on that. For example, if a brain sees that a diamond is being sold for $2,000 it will register it as $2,000 because it is a simple number.

Take away one dollar to drop the price to $1,999 and that same brain will take the number on the far left and tell you that that diamond is 1,000 and some odd dollars. That gives your brain the idea that you are saving roughly $1,000 dollars with that purchase even though they are really only saving 1/1000 of that!

Our brains automatically encode numbers extremely quickly. So quickly that it takes items into account that you don't even realize.

For example, one of the first things your brain will measure when looking at something is its size. Your brain has a universal conceptualization of size. If it is pictured bigger or written bigger it seems to become bigger in our heads. This concept of size is so embedded in our subconscious that it can sometimes create subconscious connections between visual size and numerical size even when they have no connection in the real world.

That's why customers perceive your price to be smaller if you display your price in a smaller font size.

Not $699 but $699.

You can use the reverse when it comes to discounts. You want your discounts to be as large as possible.

Not 49% OFF but **49% OFF**

A good rule of thumb to remember is that if you want it to look like a big discount, make it big. If you want to make your price seem small, then have it written small.

Shrink Costs

Another proven tip that researchers have discovered is that by removing commas from a price ($1,599 vs. $1599) it will make your price seem lower. For some this may seem to be rather silly, but there is a simple answer as to why this happens.

When you remove the comma, you reduce the number of syllables in your price:

$1,599: One-thousand five hundred and ninety-nine is 10 syllables long

$1599: Fifteen ninety-nine is only 5 syllables.

Take this sales pitch into consideration.

Customer: "How much is it?"

Jeweler: "Lucky for you it is on sale! You get it for just one thousand five hundred and ninety nine dollars! What a steal!"

Now let's take a look at the situation without that one comma standing in your way.

Customer: "How much is it?"

Jeweler: "Lucky for you it is on sale. You get it for just fifteen ninety-nine! What a steal!"

See how the price is so much smaller in comparison? The price is still the same, but you managed to make it shrink to a much more manageable number. When you talk about price with a customer, always make it smaller by removing the comma. The word "thousand" shouldn't escape your lips. Instead, stick with the eleven-ninety-nine instead.

Talk about Payments

Another way to shrink prices is by giving people the option to pay for your jewelry in small monthly installments (try saying installments instead of payments. I have a theory that it gets better traction than saying payments, but I haven't been able to put it in action just yet. Installments might take away the thought of giving away money). This takes away the large overall sum of their purchase and anchor them on the smaller monthly price.

Suppose that you're selling a solitaire diamond pendant for $799. By offering payment installments (e.g., 12 payments of $67), you taint people's comparison process. Instead of thinking about having to immediately part with nearly $800 they can just pay $67 a couple of times for the same unique piece! That sounds so much more appealing doesn't it?

Remember that people aren't stupid. Most people understand that payments eventually add up to the overall sum. Luckily, it doesn't matter because once you mention how much their monthly installments will be then those smaller numbers will be in the back of their mind. This gives it a better chance of sneaking into your customer's price comparison.

Another way to sneak into the minds of your customers a simple price is to break down cost to a daily sum and then compare it to something you buy every day, like coffee. "Your payments would be similar to buying just 8 cups of coffee a month. You can handle that can't you?"

When Should I Show Price?

When it comes to price, you need to understand which angle you are trying to accomplish. When it comes to displaying price ask yourself this question: Do I want my customer to see the product first or the price?

Much like a first impression, first exposure to prices or products influences the decisions people make. Together we are going to analyze what goes on inside the subconscious of potential buyers. When products are displayed first, our subconscious analyses a products quality deciding whether or not you like it. We can break this down mathematically.

If I see the PRODUCT then the PRICE I ask myself = Do I like this product?

When prices are displayed first, our subconscious analyses the economic value of the item before deciding whether or not an item may be favorable. We can break this down mathematically.

If I see the PRICE then the PRODUCT I will ask myself = Is this product worth it?

You want every person to base their decision on how they love the style, love the color and love that it will look good on them. You do not want them to wonder if a jewelry piece is worth a price. It will almost always be a no.

Proof of this is action in other stores can be seen at places like Tiffany's. Nowhere in their cases do they display prices of any kind. Even online their website shows their pieces in beautiful detail allowing you to fall in love with them before showing you how much money it is going to cost. Even when you click on their product their price is listed last and treated as if its unimportant. You want it so you should get it.

Show High
One of the best ways to increase your sales is to show high. It is a fact that you can influence customers to choose a more expensive option if you begin your sales presentations showing higher priced items and then working your way down. There are two reasons for this happening.

REASON 1: ANCHORING / REFERENCE PRICES
The first time you show a customer a price it anchors itself in their subconscious. From then on they will refer to that price in their mind throughout the rest of your time together. As you progress down in price the difference between your initial price that you have shown and the price you show them next will look like a better and better deal.

REASON 2: LOSS AVERSION
As human beings, we always want to win. We flaunt our success, show off our happiness and it almost kills us when we lose. If we were to do the opposite and show low to high we make it seem like the customer is losing. When you sort products by ascending price (i.e., low to high), customers view each new product as a loss in price. With each new option, they're gradually losing the ability

to pay a lower price. Thus, they feel motivated to minimize that loss by choosing a lower priced product.

But here's the flipside. When you sort products by descending price (i.e., high to low), customers view each new product as a loss in quality. Thus, they feel motivated to retain a higher quality (and more expensive) product. Emphasize your product's "top-of-the-line" raw material or any other cost-based input. That information will trigger a more empathetic perception of your price. "Our diamonds are 100%conflict free and ethically sourced"

REASON 3: ITS FLATTERING

Imagine yourself going to a car dealership to buy a new car to celebrate your promotion at work. You walk in with $20,000 in your pocket ready to buy and are greeted with a well-dressed, smiling salesman. You two hit it off immediately. There is great rapport between you two and your relationship builds to a great point. The salesman then walks you outside to show you the car the salesman pulls out a 2001 Honda Accord with bits of rust on it and a fading paint job. Wouldn't you be a little offended?

You want to spend your $20,000. It is why you are there. The same is with your customers. They want to be given the best treatment possible, and that includes being shown your best of the best. Show your customers high valued items, and then work your way into their budget.

Presenting Choices

Because you greeted you customer and built good rapport with them you should have a pretty good idea of what it is you are going to show them. The more effective you have been in any of the preceding steps, the more likely it is that one of the items you choose to present your customer will be a winner and the fewer items you'll have to show them to arrive at that final Even if you're certain you know the perfect piece, always be prepared to offer alternatives. Having choices helps the customer feel confidently in control.

Unless your customer has walked in and stated a budget then don't let prices dictate what you are going to show your customer. Never judge a person by how they look, how they talk or what they drive. Each prospect has a unique buying power that you are unaware of. Instead of imagining what they can afford, present them with pieces that will satisfy their needs and desires that you have identified that they are in need of. Research shows that customers often spend less than they plan on – or are willing to – simply because they aren't offered more expensive choices.

When a customer does express a price objection, acknowledge it, recap motives you identified in profiling, and assure him that you can satisfy the need. "I understand your concern. The good news is that the style you've described is available in a range of prices. So, let's look at something that might be a bit more comfortable."

Have Diamonds in a Range of Prices

When two diamonds share the same price, people can't immediately distinguish a difference between the two of them. As a result, they seek out negative attributes about each to find a difference instead of simply enjoying the moment. However, when you add a slight price difference, you reduce the need to search for differences. You can compound this feature by selecting diamonds that show extreme differences in either carat, cut, color, or clarify. Your customers can differentiate the products based on price alone, but the added diamond with a pronounced flaw or extreme coloring helps make that differentiation even easier to make. You can now focus more on creating a positive, emotional presentation. And that similarity makes people more likely to choose a product.

Tips

• Remember to smile throughout the showing process. You might look too serious. Remember that this is a fun.

• Mirror your customers. Mimic gestures and tone and they will begin to see you as a kindred spirit. Understand where their level is and then hype it up just enough to build the excitement.

• Use your whole body to sell, not just your words. Prospects are always on the lookout for anyone trying to swindle them out of their money, they must deal with it every day. Use your body language to build trust between the two of you.

• Maintain eye contact. Look them in the eyes throughout your presentation, but don't stare at them. It gets creepy if its too much.

• Use hand gestures with an open palm to say, 'You can trust me'.

• Facial expressions show how we really feel. Don't look all sour faced when you are describing features and benefits.

CHAPTER 9: ASKING QUESTIONS

Judge a man by his questions rather than by his answers.
Voltaire

One of the biggest mistakes salesmen make is that they talk too much. Jewelers don't make that mistake. Jewelers understand that in the grand scheme of things we ended up with two ears and one mouth. The amount we use them should be used to that same ratio; listening twice as much as we speak.

Questions
Why do we ask questions? What is the point? Is it to merely give the customer a turn to speak as we ramble? No. You ask questions to gain control of the sale. Used correctly you will even maintain that control as you move throughout your presentation. Questions allow you to gather information about a customer's needs rather than letting them hold it back or drizzle it in random statements.

Ask questions to indicate the broad areas in which you might be of service. Once you understand the area in which you can help narrow down how it is you might be able to serve them. Done correctly, you can pinpoint the exact item they desire to be shown, the repair service that they have questions about, or you can direct them to the nearest restroom.

Questions are how you are going to get the small yeses that will start the string of minor agreements and swell into a torrential river of agreement. If you get enough yesses it will become more difficult for buyers to want to say no when it is time to make a final decision.

Questions also help isolate objections. By isolating the objections that are important to an individual client you will get to the underlying reasons why a customer is interested in an item. No one is going to voice every single objection that there is in the jewelry world. Seek objections out eagerly because objections are purchasing signals.

Once you have narrowed down the objection, ask questions to answer objections. The finest way to answer an objection is with a question that, when the customer answers it, affirms that the objection is nothing to worry about or that it might even be an advantage.
    "If money was no object, would you be willing to get it today?"
    "When would be a good time to buy?"
    "Sometimes when people say X, it really means Y. Is it safe for me to assume that's the case here?"

You ask questions that determine the benefits a customer wants to own. People don't really buy products and services they buy the benefits they expect to receive from own inf those products/ services.

You ask questions to acknowledge a fact. If you say it, they can doubt you. If they say it, they must believe it is true.

You ask questions to create ownership of the object.

You ask questions to help clients rationalize decisions that they want to make. Aren't we all looking for someone to tell us that we deserve to treat ourselves? That we'll benefit from our decisions? Validation is everything. Our clients are shouting for something, we are here to offer our support.

Where to Start?

Before you ever ask a question, be sure that it is a question that they know the answer to. If they don't know the answer, they will feel stupid and attacked. Nobody likes being asked questions they don't know the answer to. Don't start off asking what carat of jewelry they are looking for. Try something more along the lines of "Are you looking for something she can wear every day or do you want it to be specifically for formal occasions?" Questions like these will lead you down a path to success. Ask questions that they have the answer to.

The questions that you will want to ask are going to be mostly open-ended. Open ended questions answer the questions who, what, when, where, why and how. If asked correctly, a customer will not be able to swing out a quick yes or no. Instead, they will have to think about how they are going to answer. When they do answer you are going to gain insight into their lives that will not only help you come closer but help you in your diamond presentations.

"Who is this for?"

"What makes her smile?"

"When was the last time you surprised her?"

"Where are you going to propose?"

"What do you think of the style?"

There is an endless list of possible questions that you

can ask in a diamond presentation. The best ones create ownership over the product, elicit emotion and keep the conversation going.

However, not all of your questions should be open ended. Asking too many open-ended questions creates an atmosphere more like an interrogation than engagement ring shopping. Closed questions are useful when you are looking to get specific answers. These pinpoint areas that may have been overlooked with your open-ended questions.

"Is that in the price range you were hoping to be in?"

"Do you like the European shank?"

Another great tool that comes with questions is your ability to offer choices. When you offer choices to a customer you give the illusion that they are in control of the sale when in reality they are dancing to your flute.

However, it is more difficult than it seems. If your options that you give them will result in a yes or no answer than 9/10 times your clients will answer with a no. The reason for this is because it is always safer to say no. They are perfectly content not buying today and if they get spooked you may have lost all the ground you have made up so far. Jewelers do not offer choices that can end in no.

One of the best times to use an alternate choice question is during follow up phone calls. For example, let's say that yesterday you had shown a diamond to a young couple who, unfortunately, didn't buy that day. However, you asked good questions, built excellent rapport, and now that you have given them 24 hours for that to sink in so you decide to call them. They answer and after exchanging pleasantries you make the mistake of saying, "When are you free to come get Anna's ring?"

Customers are never free. They are incredibly busy individuals whose schedules will always be filled to the brim with important activities if you ask when they are free. When you give them a choice, their schedule is suddenly much more open. "Jake, I have available times today and tomorrow, would it be more convenient to come in at 4 or 5 pm?" When he replies you will have your appointment and you got it because you suggested two yeses instead of a no for him to jump on.

Fast forward to during your appointment with Jake and you can use alternate choices to close your sale. These choices create ownership over the item and can have your customer knowing that they have made the right choice. You're taking them mentally to the future where they now own the item even though they haven't parted with their money yet.

"Would you like it wrapped or just in the box?"

"I can have it back by Wednesday or Thursday, which would be better for your schedule?"

If your company offers financing you can ask, "Will you be putting $300 or $400 for your down payment?". Obviously, they are going to leap on saving $100 and only putting down the $300 which is exactly what you wanted them to do.

There is one golden rule you must follow for when you ask questions. It doesn't matter how good your phrasing is or having only yes answers. If you ask the perfect question and then don't listen to the response you will fail every time. Let me reiterate this once more, if you don't actively listen to your customer you will never sell them.

LET'S TALK ABOUT TIE DOWNS
This is going to be the shortest part of this chapter, but it's got some spice you HAVE to add to your sales

presentation concoction. We are talking about tie-downs. Tie-downs are yes or no questions that are designed to get a yes for a response. Quality is important to you isn't it? Nobody is going to say no to that.

"Does that make sense?"

"And that's a nice feature, isn't it?"

"You feel that way too, don't you?"

"Saving money is important to you, isn't it?"

The most observant readers will notice that most chapter ends in a tie-down. I use them to reinforce two things. 1) I want you to agree that what you are reading is helping you learn 2) I am getting you to commit to my teachings. You will get more commitment from customers who you deliberately use tie-downs on, just as I have gotten you to commit to reading this far.

Toss tie-downs into your sales and watch as you close more sales. Why? Because by getting your customers to agree with you in small steps along the way, you have a better chance of reaching a point where they will agree to buy from you today. I think you'd agree that by using tie downs you'll get a lot more information and direction from your prospects during a close, won't you? (a shameless tie down, wasn't it? (boom, a tie-down within a tie-down)).

CHAPTER 10: TEAM SELL

*The most difficult thing is the decision to act, the rest is merely
tenacity. The fears are paper tigers. You can do anything you decide
to do. You can act to change and control your life; and the procedure,
the process is its own reward.*
Amelia Earhart

Most customers go to three brick and mortar stores
before making a purchase. If someone walks into your
store and say that this is the first place that they have
looked, do not fret. Do as you have been taught. Greet
and connect, show high, build rapport and educate. Once
you discover that this is the very first store that they have
looked in, take that tidbit of information and keep it in the
back of your mind. Why? Because you are going to need to
call in backup. This is called a T.O or a turnover of the sale
from you to another associate.

What you are doing when you call in someone for a
T.O what you are doing is you are giving that customer a
new shopping experience. Now, instead of having to go to
another brick and mortar store to look around, your

customer is having a new shopping experience right in your store. The salesperson who takes over could even show them the exact same pieces that you showed, but it will be a fresh start to what your store has to offer. They won't need more shopping experiences because you will have already given it to them.

Furthermore, T. O's are great because they help you get to underlying issues that customers are too scared to tell you. As you show them jewelry pieces you are building a relationship. Eventually you are going to get to a point where your customer doesn't want to hurt that relationship by telling you the complete truth. For example, say that they love a ring, but it is outside their budget. Instead of telling you, they keep it to themselves. How can you help them if they aren't telling you their needs? That is what a T.O is for.

A good T.O. means a fresh start for the customer. Their walls are down because of the rapport you built and now your fellow jeweler can ask the hard questions right off the bat.

"What rings have you really fallen in love with? Oh, you love this one? What's holding you back from getting it today? Do you want to see what it looks like on someone's hand?"

This way, the customer is almost required to tell you their true thoughts. It doesn't matter if they have already seen everything that your store has to offer, a good T.O is going to help you close the sale today.

Beyond giving your shoppers new experiences, it also allows you to show your sincerity and honesty. For example, at one point in a diamond presentation a customer may ask a question that you do not know the answer to. Do not guess or give them any false information. You are an honest and educational jeweler who has integrity above all else. Instead of making guesses, turn to one of your associates who you believe will be able to help you.

Just because T.O's are fantastic doesn't mean you should whistle someone over as soon as possible. Give your client time to look around and show them the best your store has to offer. Build that relationship with them and try to sell your jewelry today. Then, when your customer begins to become excited or seem to become lost initiate a T.O.

How to Initiate a T.O

One of the most important things to keep in mind when initiating a TO is that your customer must not feel that they are being abandoned or given up on. They must believe that there is a legitimate reason that another person has entered the conversation. Make it feel/seem like the most logical and natural thing in the world.

For example, you may notice that your customer begins to seem disheartened that you can't seem to find a necklace for a birthday. This is a great time to call in a TO with your associate named Alex. Here are four great ways to bring Alex into the sale.

"Let me grab Alex really quick, she is our necklace expert."

"Alex, do we happen to still have _____ in the store? (wait for them to say yes or no) We are looking for a special birthday gift, what would you want if it was your birthday?"

"For this next necklace I want to show you what this necklace looks like when someone is wearing it. Alex, could I borrow you for a second to be a model?"

"I don't know the answer to that question, but Alex happens to be our diamond guru. Let me grab her real quick."

The reason for bringing in another person should be believable. It should not diminish the original salesperson abilities in the eyes of the customer, and it should be viewed as a benefit to have this new jeweler assist them.

Let's also reverse the roles. Say that you notice a fellow sales associate is struggling and it looks like they could use some backup in a presentation. Do not just barge in and take over. These are your co-workers and you want to build an atmosphere of cooperation and mutual respect for each other's sales abilities. Insert yourself as a support character as if it was the only natural thing to do.

The number one way to put yourself in a position to T.O is to offer a free service to customers.

"I am sorry to interrupt, but I was wondering if you would like me to clean your jewelry for free while you are here?"

"I am sorry to interrupt, but I was wondering if you would like a free beverage."

This gives your associate the chance to ask for help. If they do not, then at the very least you have reset the situation by allowing both parties to no longer focus on the sales presentation.

Have a signal, eye contact, ask for an opinion, call in a favor. It doesn't matter how you T.O as long as you T.O. Make the commitment to T.O every sale that is not being closed. It is always better to take 50% or even 30% of a sale than to get nothing, don't you agree? Put aside any petty issues you might have with Harold and get him to come help close your sale. Do yourself a favor and put yourself into a position where you can be listening to others give diamond presentations and wait to be T.O'd in.

It is your responsibility to prepare yourself to be T.O'd just as much as it is your responsibility to get a T.O partner.

Would you rather do your calculus homework alone or in a group setting? It's the same with sales. Getting multiple people to review the process, understand the current situation, and work together towards a positive outcome has huge advantages.

T.O Rules

When you T.O someone into a sale there are three basic rules that you need to follow:

1. Don't tell the person you T.O'd any objections.
2. Don't count out the newbies
3. Don't T.O to the competition

#1 When you are handing off the sale to another associate, it needs to be a fresh start. Don't tell your partner what your customer is looking for. Let the customer explain what it is they need. This is because humans naturally don't want to feel stupid. Say that you showed your customer a ring and they told you they didn't like it. Well, maybe five minutes later it is all they can think about. They aren't going to tell you that they changed their mind because that will make them feel stupid, or guilty because they somehow lied to you. However, when you T.O someone into the sale, your customer is free to say how they truly feel.

Let your customer reset and re-evaluate how they feel. Don't tell them how they feel, let them explain themselves to your T.O partner.

#2 It is okay to T.O to fresh faces on your team. They need the experience and you can both benefit from working together as they will bring in new insights into the sale. They may be exactly what you needed to close your sale today.

#3 Don't T.O to the competition means two things. First, it means that you should never let a customer leave your store empty handed without T.O'ing someone. Maximize your success by giving your customer more in-store experiences and do your best to close every sale today.

Secondly, don't recommend your customer to another jeweler. Ever. You are the best. You can sell them on what you have in stock. Just because some other store has a style you know your customer will like doesn't mean you can't help them fall in love with what you have in your store. Trust in your team's sales abilities. Together you can close them.

When to Initiate a T.O
During greet and connect:
After trying a couple of times to connect and make contact but fail. T.O.

While showing:
After showing more than five pieces with no positive feelings toward what you are showing. TO. Don't let your customer get antsy. If you don't find something soon they may even lose interest.

Commitment Building:
You found the piece they love but need some help to get to a higher level of commitment. Excitement level should be rising. This is where your customers will raise objections. What if it doesn't fit? Do you have financing? What if she doesn't like it?

Same Objection:

'I really like it but... I want to keep looking around.' After a while, the customer may no longer trust your ability to find them what they are looking for. If this is the case turn it over. Sometimes, they are doing this because they are simply afraid of saying no. Sometimes they are just scared to look foolish in front of you or don't understand something that you have explained to them. Instead of asking for clarification they object. Adding another person to the equation and giving them some space allows for them to relax and be more honest.

IMPORTANT

Before they let anyone walk out of the store without buying, always introduce customers to an associate. The second employee might have a new angle on the sale or make a different kind of personal connection. This also gives the original rep time to pop into the back to fetch a new piece while the customer is preoccupied. No matter what, customers should always speak to at least two people before leaving your store.

Sometimes you won't T.O for help, but because your customer does not like you. Don't take these situations personally. It usually has nothing to do with your looks, your abilities or how you greeted them. Prospects who cross paths with you may not like you simply because you are the first person that they saw in your store. Remember, buying jewelry is a big commitment and they are trying to express a lot of emotions that they usually keep to themselves.

To combat this, most people will come into your store with a wall up to protect themselves. Most of the time, a great greet and connect with good rapport building will put your customers at ease allowing you to hit it off. However, there are times where that will not be enough. Sometimes your personalities will clash, and it may be difficult to get off on the right foot. Other times it may simply be that your customer prefers to work with people of a certain gender when it comes to jewelry. Maybe you remind them of a person that they hated back in high school. The possibilities are endless so there is no reason to take being disliked personally. Unless you didn't take my deodorant advice and smell like a pig, it is usually not your fault.

Control What You Can Control

In situations where the customers don't like you, be aware that it is happening. It is easy to recognize when there is a good vibe happening between you and your customer. They will act like they enjoy your company. They will look you in the eye, smile, and laugh at all the incredible proposal jokes you tell. You will notice that they will listen carefully to what it is that you have to say and will occasionally ask questions for clarification.

Customers will act very differently if they have negative feelings. They will not look you in the eyes and will often focus on the case in front of you. They won't talk much and when they do their responses are short and lack any personal details. They may even completely ignore you or question your intelligence. Once you have recognized the situation that you are in the next step is incredibly easy, turn your sale over to another one of your jewelers. It is always better to take the safe route and turn it over to another one of your associates than to try to win them over. Increase your chances of success by giving your customers a fresh start with a new associate who may not remind them of their high school ex-sweetheart.

Customers buy from people that they like and trust. It is far better to try a new start with a fresh face than it is to claw your way up from the bottom. Don't beat yourself up for not being loved by everyone. It is impossible to accomplish that. You should be eager and excited that you gave it your all and now you have drastically improved your chances of success by encouraging your associates to help you out.

CHAPTER 11: OBJECTIONS

Predicting rain doesn't count. Building arks does.
Warren Buffett

When a jeweler envisions their next sale, they often do it with fantastic optimism. They envision a couple who are deeply in love skipping through your store's front door. You happily greet them and build some genuine rapport. You discover that they are looking to get engaged and use your stage tools to involve your love-struck couple physically, emotionally and mentally. They applaud your skills and whip out their wallets to sign on the dotted line. You have successfully sold them their dream ring without any hiccups. What a dream right?

And that is what it is, a dream. Your customers are going to have a concern or two. Don't let that scare you. Only serious buyers voice their concerns by having an objection here or there. If the person you are showing isn't objecting during your presentation you are either not attempting to sell them, they aren't listening, or they are not serious buyers. If they are doing any of those things, then they aren't going to sign the dotted line and you are wasting your time.

So how do you handle those pretty little things called objections? If you build good rapport with a customer, learn everything you can about them, and gain their trust, that's the best way to overcome potential objections before they arise. This means listening and observing; learning all you can about a customer; knowing your products and services inside and out; and most of all, being yourself. People can see right through someone who adopts an artificial "sales personality." I find that for customers who have a strong relationship with a retailer, most objections are not as serious as they could be.

In the diamond industry objections are nothing more than ways your customers are slowing things down. They do this to keep themselves from making a rash decision. To keep themselves from being "sold" you might say. Objections are going to be seen in every presentation that you'll attempt to make. Accept this fact and you'll open your mind to the ways that will allow you to handle, address, and overcome objections.

Until you can come to terms with objections, you are not going to reach your full potential. The greatest jewelers love hearing even the pickiest of objections. They know that they've reached the Klondike and are digging for gold when they start hearing objections. Objections are the rungs of the ladder to sales success.

Once you have climbed to the top of the ladder, they own what you are selling. There is not any other way to sell a customer except by grasping and overcoming the most common concerns of those customers. If you decide to overcome objections by learning the material in this book, you'll learn to love objections because they announce buying intention and point the way to closing the sale.

So, what is an objection? An objection is a statement by potential clients that they want to know more. Of course, objections don't usually come out sounding like a polite request for additional information. People aren't trying to make it easy for you. They usually are sincerely objecting-they just don't realize they're just asking for more information. It's your job to know that they need more, and to know what to do about it. In short, objections are really buying signals—the customer is saying they want to buy, but they need a problem solved first.

Most Common Objections

Most objections are simply defense mechanisms that customers use to regain control of the sale. When a potential buyer raises an objection, they are trying to slow things down. They do intend to buy; they just want the time to think things over before taking the next step in the sales process. This may be that they are still unsure on some level that what you have is what they want to buy. Maybe they have some need that they didn't know they had pop into their mind. Maybe they aren't telling you the full truth. Whatever the reason may be, it doesn't matter. Whenever someone raises an objection it is a buying signal.

You don't necessarily have to address every objection that your customer throws at you. Some people see selling situations as opportunities to debate. They'll toss objections at you all day long if you let them. When selling couples, you'll have one of them start to go along with your presentation and the other one will suddenly start objecting and fighting you. Sometimes the other spouse, the one who is going along with you, is more surprised than you are. The fighting spouse will usually just want to catch his/her breath or make sure that you can answer their minor objections eloquently before things get any thicker.

Handling Objections
1.Hear Them Out

Far too many jewelers leap on an objection before the other person has a chance to finish saying it. The prospect barely gets five words out- and already the salesperson is yammering away as though the evil thing will multiply unless its stomped out immediately. 'I gotta make him wrong quick or he won't buy from me' seems to be their panicky reaction to the first hint of any objection.

Not only will the prospect feel irritated to be interrupted, but they will also feel pushed, and uneasy. 'Why's the salesperson jumping on that so fast and so hard?' your prospect will ask himself. They will smell a rat. Maybe you even raise an objection that they hadn't thought of in your rush to squash one they did ask. How embarrassing.

2. Feed the Objection Back

This is one of the best techniques for getting them to answer their own objection. It works especially well with married couples. I've often fed the objection back to the husband and then sat back as the wife hopped on it and closed him for me. To feed a concern back to potential clients, all you need to do is repeat it back to them with a sincere questioning tone in your voice.

"I don't have any money"

"You don't have any money?"

"Well, I only have $1,000 to spend."

"That is great! With that kind of a down payment you can buy anything in this store!"

"I didn't know that you had financing options. I've been trying to build my credit."

3. Question the Concern

Ask them to elaborate on or clarify their concern. Do it seriously. Avoid any hint of sarcasm, impatience or contempt. If you really get into the details of their objection, they'll feel a strong pull toward removing it from themselves. Even if it doesn't happen, while the prospects are expounding further on their objection, you will have more time to decide what course of action will be the best to overcome it. It will feel very similar to the scenario you had above.

4. Answer the Objection

You might sarcastically think, "Gee, thanks for nothing you stupid book. That really helps me out." Don't worry-I'm going to show you how. Have you ever stared at the ceiling in the dark of night thinking about all the objections that prospects could hit at you? Sometimes it seems like they have their own objection creation training program to learn every negative that can possibly be raised. Some salespeople strike one objection they can't seem to overcome, and it gives them nightmares.

Here's how it works. The crunchier the objection is on their mind when they go into every meeting or walk up to every potential client. They don't know when or even if that wipeout objection will strike- but they can't get it out of their thoughts. So, the tension builds until it is too great. Without realizing it, the sales associate unwillingly starts dropping hints that cause the prospect to bring up the concern they dread most.

Throughout your career, everything you sell will have a few features or weaknesses that you wish it didn't have. There will always be something that can turn into a cruncher objection if you let it prey on your mind.

Professional jewelers will study the weak points their pieces have, and they learn how to handle the situation. They often do this by admitting the disadvantage and immediately comparing it with an advantage. "Yes, white gold does need more maintenance, but our free service plan covers all of that for the next 100 years."

5. Confirm the Answer

Don't reply to the objection and then move on in the presentation. Your customers may not have understood you or maybe they stopped listening before you finally covered the point because they thought of something else. Always allow for the possibility that people who are close to a decision may get a little overwhelmed with information. After you've answered the objection in a way you feel should overcome it, confirm that you have. Ask questions like:

"That clarifies this point, don't you agree."

"That's the answer you're looking for isn't it".

"With that question out of the way we can go ahead don't you think?"

"That settles things doesn't it?"

Your customers will let you know if they need more clarity or if they are ready to move on.

6. Change Gears

Immediately go to the next step in your selling sequence or on to the next objection they raise. You may end up repeating these six steps two or three times if you are working with someone who likes to object. Once you're good at your job, you'll eliminate many objections in advance with your preplanned questions and smooth presentations- designed to do just that. Once you have confirmed that you've overcome an objection move on.

To signal that the last step is over and that you'll be going on to the next step, use body language as you speak. That is, make an appropriate gesture, look or step in a new direction, turn the page of your diamond pamphlet, introduce the next step with a phrase such as, "by the way…" Let's review the six steps to handling objections:

(1) hear it
(2) feed it
(3) question it
(4) answer it
(5) confirm it
(6) move on with it

Make this your standard method for addressing every concern. Learn this material and it'll be better for your energy than any sleeping pill can buy. You won't fear the bedbugs and nightmares of objections any longer.

Here are some of the most common objections that you are going to come across.

I am going to bring her back and let her choose.

He is simply afraid. He has been burned in the past and lacks the confidence to make his own decisions. He is willing to forgo romance for safety.

(1) Hear them out: David, you certainly could bring her back.

(2) Feed the objection back: I could show her around and help her find something she may want and I may even get her excited about a piece.

(3) Question the objection: But I won't be able to do one thing, do you know what that is?

(4) Answer the objection: I won't be able to make a romantic moment for her. Something that she will cherish forever. If you bring her back, you will only be giving her a ring.

(5) Confirm the answer: Wouldn't you rather give her the ring and the memory?

(6) Move on with a gesture: Hand him the ring and be absolutely silent. Let what you have said sink in and let him sell himself.

What if she doesn't like it?

(1) Hear them out: I understand that you might be a little scared to get her something.

(2) Feed the question back: She's not only going to like it; she is going to love it.

(3) Question the objection: Do you know why?

(4) Answer the objection: Because it is coming from you.

(5) Confirm the answer: She is going to love it.

(6) Move on with a gesture: What do you say we wrap this up really nice for her? Would you like it with a bow or without?

I don't want to buy it while she is here. I want to surprise her.

(1) Hear them out: I know how you feel, these kinds of things should definitely be a surprise.

(2&3) Feed the question back/Question the objection: Wouldn't she be surprised to see this, the ring of her dreams, on her finger?

(4) Answer the objection: If you really want to surprise her, get her the ring she wants. The ring she has dreamed of and get it for her today.

(5) Confirm the answer: If you don't get it for her she is going to be waiting for it every single day, and that is torture. You said it yourself, she is the nicest girl you have ever met, but each day she goes without her ring she is going to get angrier and scarier.

(6) Move on with a gesture: So, what do you say, will you make her happy today or make her keep waiting?

If he still is set in his thoughts that he wants to surprise her then now is a perfect time for a TO. One of your co-workers can take her to the other side of the room leaving you and your customer alone. You can then do paperwork, send the ring off to be sized and close the sale all without their future partner knowing what you are doing. Just because you are sitting down and doing paperwork doesn't mean that they are buying today (even though they are) so it is easy to still have everything be a surprise.

I want to look around/ this is the first place I have looked.

(1) Hear them out: I totally understand that you would want to shop around

(2) Feed the Question back: How many stores are you going to visit before you have felt like you have shopped around?

(3) Question the objection: Do you really need to look around more?

(4) Answer the objection: I ask because this is something that you know you like and it's in the price range you are looking for.

(5) Confirm the answer: This necklace is what you have been looking for and now you have found it.

(6) Move on with a gesture: So are you going to follow fate and get something you know you love at a price you can afford or waste your time "shopping".

I want to think about it.

Whenever you hear a prospect say that they want to take some time to think before they buy, they don't really want to think about this purchase. What they are saying is that there is an objection that they haven't raised yet. More often than not it has nothing to do with style or quality-- it is the price. This is when you need to pinpoint exactly why they want to look around. You can handle this with a question takedown.

QUESTION DOWN

Let's say that a couple walks into your retail store and settle by one of your ruby necklaces. When they ask questions, you give your demonstration and learn two things. They are Mr. and Mrs. Jones and they want that necklace. You go through a few closes with no success and then Mr. Jones says,

"Thanks for your time. We'll think about it and let you know."

What does, "I'll let you know" really mean in cases like this?

It means, now that they've found what they want, and they're going to shop around and see if they can buy it any cheaper. Remember, always lead them towards answering their own objections.

"That's a wise decision Mr. Jones. I'd like to ask you a couple of questions before you go. Were you impressed with the style of the ruby necklace?"

"Oh yes"

"And it is the deep shade of red you are looking for?"

"Well yeah, it's about right"

Gently list all the thing that they were pleased with. As you do this work in very briefly all the positive things you can: we service everything we sell, we have free delivery, we offer liberal credit terms. In a few cases you'll be able to close them by striking a responsive chord with some of the services that you can offer. If not, you'll be able to get down to the final objection, which almost always is money. When you get them to agree that the reason they won't buy right now is money, you've isolated your challenge.

Objection Areas

Objections happen based on three areas: Quality, Style and Price.

1. Price

"It's too much money."

"I was looking for something less expensive."

"When is your next sale?"

"How much if I pay cash today?"

You are going to hear these all day long, every day. Remember, just because the customer raises a question about the price it doesn't mean he is objecting to the price. He is trying to slow the sale down and rationalize if he is paying a fair price. He wants to be reassured If he believes that the item isn't worth that price, then you haven't sold him enough on quality. This is where your romancing comes in. Every piece of jewelry in your store is just waiting to be reminded as to why they are special. Why they are valuable.

"Yes, it is definitely worth $1599. What you are getting is what the Greeks thought were the tears of the gods resting on one of the most precious metals known to man. Look at it closely and see how it turns the light into rainbows, that is because ..."

2. Quality
Quality objections are easily confused with price objections.

"I saw that somewhere for less money."

"I can get a better color for the same price."

"My friend can get it cheaper."

These are not price objections, but quality objections. Don't jump right into trying to sell them on the price by bashing your competitors. Talk about differences that could account for the price difference. For example, with diamonds of the biggest differences in price is the Cut. Remember, the cut makes up 60% of its price. Discuss your company history and what makes you different, better, special. All the customer is interested in is the benefits he receives for giving you his hard-earned money. Make sure that you can do all of this and not mention price.

"I saw the same diamond on the internet for half that

price."

"That is very smart of you to do your research on diamonds because it is a very important purchase. Each diamond is very unique, and it can be very difficult to distinguish them without seeing them side by side. The diamond you are holding happens to be of exquisite craftsmanship.

"Hold it up into the light. Gaze into the dazzling fireworks show that she is going to see on her hand every single day. Our company has a diamond guarantee that covers any damage that that diamond may sustain. We replace it for life if it is ever stolen. You have five years of goldsmith service that is all in house. Buying your diamond with us guarantees that what you see today is what you get and we promise to keep it that way forever."

This may sound like a good reason for buying, but it doesn't directly answer the question of why the other diamond is half the price. Just giving the above answer will leave your customer thinking.

"So, they have been doing this for a while, there is a warranty and the diamond is pretty. Is that worth oh so many dollars? I don't think so."

In order for the above situation to end well the other diamond must be questioned and interrogated. Or you need to show why this diamond is different, better, special before going into the above answer. If you don't address quality first you are going to be attempting to sell your history, services and guarantees for the difference in price. In most cases, that is not enough. People will think that you are using that history, services and guarantees to jack up your prices. This is why people have price objections. They are testing the waters to see if there are any justifications as to why something cost so many dollars.

Overcome quality objections by noting craftsmanship. Point out how meticulously a migraine edge is made by hand. Let them notice how all your diamonds are matched so that there are no obstructions to observing its whole beauty. Make sure that you not only know but believe that the reasons as to why you and the piece you are selling is different, better, special.

Once you believe in that, tell your customers confidently and enthusiastically how you are different, better, special. If you do all this, you are letting the customers feel comfortable that you are selling quality items at fair prices. They aren't being ripped off and they aren't going to have any bad feelings after they have bought.

So, what if you are on the flipside? Instead, you are the one competing against the big shot in town. They have the more recognizable brands, they have been around longer, and their sales staff is a well-oiled machine. If that is the case you may be asked, "Why is this so much cheaper than___? Why is it so much less? They offer a lot of warranties and service that you don't.

For obvious reasons, you must tell them the honest to God truth as to why your prices are so much less. You have a smaller profit margin.

"Why are your prices so much less than your competitors?"

"That is one of my favorite questions. You see, we are local and always have been. Since we are local, we price things way lower so that our friends and neighbors can get the absolute best quality at the lowest costs."

Boom. You overcame that quality objection like a champ. You are a hometown hero trying to get the best stuff at the lowest price and the customer will love that about you. Share your excitement about how you are already saving them money just by walking in the door. Branded jewelers usually have more costs to pay and have large overheads to worry about. Use their size to their advantage and you will be able to take down anyone.

Well, what about their warranties? We can't offer those. Well, there is something that you have that a lot of others don't. You are going to give personal, local service. The big bad jewelers of the world have surprisingly high turnover rates, but you, you stick to your guns and you are in it for the long haul. You will know your customers in's and out's while the other guy is only going to know them by a number.

Use your customers intuitive perception that big companies have quality goods that are overpriced to your advantage. Get creative. You know who you are and how your business fits into the surrounding areas mold. Find those things that are going to make you different, better, special and sell them on quality over and over again.

3. Style objections
These kinds of objections are sometimes the trickiest ones to detect without actively searching for them. "I'll know it when I see it." "Let me browse for a second." "This one just isn't speaking to me." What are your customers really trying to tell you? They are trying to tell you in the politest way possible that they don't like it. Plain and simple. Sometimes, the reason that they don't love it is because of the price, but that is a price objection that you are going to overcome. This kind of "I don't like it" is because the style isn't what they think they want.

The best way to detect if they love the style is to watch their face. Are they focusing in on the ring and slowly sprouting a smile? Or are they eyes wandering around your store? Do you feel like they are leaning towards the glass, or away from it? Can you feel the connection or is there some disconnect?

If you feel like it is any of the second half of each question, then you have yourself an objection of style. This is where I tell all my salesmen and saleswomen the most important thing that they need to know about selling jewelry.

You customer doesn't know what they want.
You have what they want. You just need to sell it.

Think about it for a second. Every customer of yours who has walked in your door has no clue what he/she wants. How often has someone walked into your store and proclaims their love that they have for white gold princess cut diamond engagement rings and then winds up leaving with a 14k rose gold oval ring? Customers don't know what they want.

They don't know that they want a European shank until they get to try one on and are told the benefit of not having it spin on their finger (the number on issue women have with rings). Your prospects don't know that they will need to have their white gold rings rhodium flashed ever couple of years or so and that you will provide them that service for free. They don't know that they are in love with a ring. They are caught up in the whirlwind of choices in a world where there are even more choices around every corner.

That is why you cannot ask them what they are looking for.

You read that right. You cannot ask a customer what color of golf they are looking for even though it feels like the natural thing for you to ask. Fight that feeling. That is what the average diamond salesman will ask. You are not average. When you ask white or yellow gold you are limiting the choices that are available to your customer. When your customer answers with yellow gold you can no longer show them your large inventory of white and rose gold items. You can argue that they didn't even want to see it in the first place and that is why they answered with white gold. I argue back with a simple question, how many times has a customer fallen in love with an item that they at first had no desire to see?

You need to be excited about showing your customer your entire assortment of choices. Give them the physical, mental and emotional involvement that they are craving for in a jewelry sale. Learn exactly what it is that they do like and find out what they do not like.

Don't do "shotgun showmanship" where you pull out each piece and go. How about this one? This one? This one? That is just pelting your customer with the option of saying no. Plus, it is not personal in the slightest. Really show them that you care by carefully selecting each piece that you show them.

If a customer doesn't like a piece, find out the reasoning behind it. Wait until they say something like 'it's not my favorite' and then ask them what would you change about it to make it yours? Then you must actively listen to what it is they say next. Use the information that they give you so that you will know exactly what piece it is that you will show them next.

Each piece you show is going to become more in sync with what she desires on the inside. Pinning pictures of rings on Pinterest is one thing. Trying jewelry on in the store with a talented jeweler putting pieces that reflect the purchaser's deep inner motions is quite another.

You don't just want the customer to fall in love with an engagement ring. You want them to fall in love with this engagement ring. Sure, there may be hundreds of other styles that are similar, but you should make them want to buy this one.

Overcoming: What if he gives me a ring and I don't like it? (from the perspective of someone who was just proposed to)

Sometimes, you will have someone who doesn't like the ring that they were proposed to with, but they don't know how to tell their future spouse that they don't like it. When this happens, you need to be prepared to give the best possible answer to retain your customer and your relationship with them.

Tell your customer something along the following lines:

"Rachel, you aren't alone in this. Future husbands want to start off the relationship right by surprising you with that ring, but sometimes they don't get the style exactly right. He wants to show you how much he loves you. When you start to bring up how you may want to exchange your ring, you need to keep the focus on that love.

"Begin by telling him how much you love him. Let him know how much it means to you that he did what he did. Focus on his love and then give him the chance to make you even happier by getting a style that you have dreamed of. You can come in and exchange it at any time. When you do, I will be here to help you get what it is you need so that you can both be as happy as possible."

No matter what you say, never speak negatively about the ring that they are wearing. Tell your customers to keep the focus on the act of love that comes with the giving of the gift. Do that, and they can get something that they like with as little effort as possible.

Improving on Overcoming Objections

The fastest way to improve is to go and make a list of objections along with their responses. Once you make your list, you are going to need to practice them until you start singing them in the shower. Go over a new one every single day and imagine all the possible scenarios that can come out of them. You can even bring in a fellow associate and do some role-play to get fresh ideas and do more actual presentations.

Being able to overcome objections is what is going to separate the goods from the greats. You have the mindset needed to become a true jeweler and have mastered the fundamentals necessary to be in control of the sale. Your success isn't luck and it most certainly isn't just a good streak. You are becoming better. You are becoming a champion, and champions practice their objections, right.

CHAPTER 12: CLOSES

Permanence, perseverance and persistence in spite of all obstacles, discouragements, and impossibilities: It is this, that in all things distinguishes the strong soul from the weak.
Thomas Carlyle

A professional jeweler's job and responsibility is to ask for the sale no matter what. It doesn't matter the type of sales presentation you have given or how terrible a job you think you have done in the selling process. Always ask for the sale. It may seem obvious, but look at what usually happens below:

20% of the time - The salesperson tries to close the sale.
20% of the time- Client says, "I'll take it"
60% of the time- No attempt is made to close the sale.

It is clear that most salespeople don't ask for the sale comes from a fear of rejection or that they don't feel that they have earned the right to ask the customer to purchase the jewelry. Let me assure you that if you have followed the sales process as described, you have earned the right to ask the customer to buy.

The reason customers don't buy today is because they are paralyzed with indecision. It isn't their lack of money or not knowing if they will buy. They lack knowing where they will buy. Why should they buy from you? What makes you different, better or special? Your answer to this can't be generic. Better prices, better service and better quality are things that you can see plastered on every storefront. These have basically lost their value in the public's eye.

You need solid, specific reasons for your customers to choose why they should buy from you. For example, I worked with a company that was one of the oldest companies in Utah. That is the feature. Telling that to a customer is cool, but it means little to nothing to them without telling them the benefit from buying from a company who is older than sliced bread. You need to add a benefit. That benefit could be any number of things like having the best vendors to choose from, getting to hand select the best quality items on the market or anything you believe will be beneficial from the customer since you built rapport. You could say something like this:

"Our company has been around for over a hundred years and we are nationwide. That means that we are going to take care of you, and Anna's ring no matter where life takes you."

If you come from a smaller store that may only have one location you can say something like, "Our company hand selects each piece that we bring in assuring that what we give to you is something we would take home ourselves."

Once you have established that you are different, better, special you have built a foundation for them to want to buy from you that they will not hear anywhere else. Sprinkle these reasons throughout your diamond presentations to build on that foundation. They won't remember everything you say, but they will know when they are feeling like they are in the right place.

Emotions That Close Sales

When you ask for the sale, try as hard as you can to have your customer feel a sense of urgency. Urgency is what is going to be the difference between purchasing today and walking out the door with nothing. There are three emotions that you can use to build urgency in your customer.

1. Scarcity
2. Fear of Loss
3. Personal Reward

Scarcity-

"This is the last one in the company"

"No other store carries it."

"The designer only makes 120 of these a year."

Fear of Loss-

"This is the lowest the price has ever been."

"Deciding now vs. next week is the difference of $500 on the bottom line. Would you rather pay that $500 or just go ahead and do it? I mean you like the ring, don't you (boom tie-down)?"

"You really should take advantage of the tremendous savings. You want to get this at the best price, don't you (great use of a tie-down)?"

Personal Rewards-

"Haven't you waited long enough? You deserve it treat yourself."

"Guys, this is it. I cannot get you a better price than right now. Do you wanna pull the trigger and get that deal?"

"If you commit to buy now, I can fast track you to the front of the repair queue. We can have this sized and on her finger by tonight."

Once your customer feels the sense of urgency, it is time to start using your closing techniques. Closing techniques are simply different methods of asking questions in order to complete the sale. Whether it is straightforward and direct, or subtle and reserved, the point is you must ask for the sale. What is the first close you need in your repertoire? How about I give you four.

The Ask-For-It Close:

This is a relatively self-explanatory close. It is a technique where you simply ask for the sale. It can be worded in a variety of ways, but the method is very straightforward. For example:

"What do you think?"

"Let's write it up?"

"I know this will be perfect. Let's do it?"

Or you can do it by asking it in the form of a question where answering yes to either option means that they are taking it home today.

"Would you like me to gift wrap this for you or would you like to wrap it yourself?"

"Would you like to pay for this with cash, check or credit card?" The

Question Reflection Close:

This is when a customer shows a buying sign like, "Can we get this ring sized by Friday?" The jeweler should answer the question and then reflect the question back as a close. For example: "I am sure we can have it sized for you by Friday. What time on Friday would you like to pick it up?" Without the closing question you haven't asked for the sale, you have simply answered the customer's question and then tying it to the sale. Don't leave the customer hanging, close the deal.

The Say Nothing Close:

In jewelry sales, you have the unique opportunity to allow the customer to stare at the piece and hold onto it in your shop as long as she wants. Other big-ticket items such as cars and houses cannot be held in the buyer's hands. Once you have presented the product, you hand it to the customer and say nothing. Let them look it over, see it in their hands and even try it on. In some cases, the jewelry will just sell itself. All you have to do is to stand there and look pretty. It can sometimes be for long periods of time. Wait until your customer says something. Do not interrupt their silence.

The Benefit-Review Close:

This is where you summarize all the benefits in a couple of sentences followed by asking for the sale. This is a great close for many selling situations. It may even be the appropriate close for a prospect from whom you haven't been getting very good indicators in the presentation process. We all know the type of people to which I am referring. You give an enthusiastic, no-holds-barred diamond demo, and all you get back is, "Eh!" There is no excitement or enthusiasm. One of the only things you can then do is to review what they told you they needed and what you can give the, reworded as a closing question.

For example: "Based on everything that we have discussed, I know that he will love the versatility of the two-tone band, and the durability of the sapphire crystal, not to mention the beauty of the watch itself. She is going to absolutely love this watch. Let's write it up for her?"

Go out into the world of the internet and find some more closes to add to your repertoire as you build up your skills. Keep in mind, however, that you don't need to know all the fancy ways of getting people to buy. All you need to remember, is to ask for the sale. Always be asking for the sale.

Trial Closes

All throughout your presentation you should be using a closing technique called a trail close. Trial closes are extremely valuable and low risk. The difference between a trial close and an actual close is that a trail close asks for an opinion while a close asks for a decision. Your trial close is a measurement, not a commitment. You measure where they are at, it's the best tool for probing customer's interests. It's like a recipe and you are checking to see if the oven is hot enough or if the noodles are still hard?

Boiled down to their core, trail closes are just open-ended questions asking for opinions. For example:

"How do you feel about what we have discussed so far?"

"What do you think about the shape of the center diamond?"

"Based on what you've heard so far, what are your questions?"

"If you had your way, what changes would you make to this ring?"

"When we first met you mentioned [something]. Could you tell me a little more about that?"

Sprinkle these open-ended questions throughout your presentation to help you assess where your customers are in the sales process. The response you get from your trial closing questions will tell you what to do/show next. Using trial closing questions will improve your diamond presentations quicker than any other tool in a jeweler's set of techniques

Buying Signals

Throughout your presentations keep a watchful eye out for buying signals. Buying signals are the actions prospective buyers take that may indicate they're close to making a purchasing decision. You will notice that your customers go from mild expressions of interests to a much more focused desire when you start getting close to finishing a sale. These are great times to ask for the sale repeatedly. Don't shy away. They want to buy; they just need to be asked. So, if they are giving you buying signals keep asking for the sale until they say yes. You will pick up on most buying signals naturally, but we are also going to look at some more obscure signals.

Pricing Questions

Price and discount-related questions can be misleading. If these questions come up at the beginning of the sales conversation, it's possible the prospect is overly focused on cost rather than value. But if the prospect has gotten the opportunity to realize the product's value, asking about price suggests they're going to buy soon.

"Do you offer financing?"

"Are there any discounts available"

Positive Statements

This is when customers talk and act like they already own the piece you are showing. You should continually be giving your customers positive statements about the jewelry, but when it comes from them that is when they are telling you that they want to own that item.

"This will fit well into her wardrobe"

"She has a dress that would go stunning with that."

Service and Delivery Dates

Once a buyer has moved into the decision stage and determined they're interested in a particular piece, they start thinking about logistics: Do we have to bring it to this store to get the diamonds inspected? Can you deliver it to my house, or do I have to pick it up? Disinterested or less committed prospects, on the other hand, are far less concerned with details. Interested buyers want to know all the facts. For that reason, reps should keep their ears perked for questions like:

"How long would sizing and setting take after we sign?"

"Would it be possible to get it made by January?"

"What are your service plan options?"

Expressions of Desire

To motivate prospects to act, reps should paint a picture of the jewelry piece in their world and the reactions it will get from people. Salespeople will know this picture has taken hold if prospects start discussing it of their own accord. For instance, a prospect who's beginning to want to purchase gives statements like:

"This could be what we're looking for."

"It would be great to have this for the wedding."

"She would love me forever if I got her this."

"Kendra would literally die/scream."

Risk-Minimization Questions

Sometimes a customer is leaning toward buying but wants to cover their bases first. These are the people that have been burned in the past, and don't want it to happen again. In these cases, they'll ask one or two questions that'll help them feel more comfortable with the purchase. These questions usually sound similar to:

"If she doesn't like it, what happens?"

"Do you have a satisfaction-guaranteed policy?"

"What's your interest rate like?"

"How long does your warranty last?"

Next Step Questions

Successful salespeople lay out clear next steps at every

stage of the process. However, prospects who are eager to buy will often preempt this conversation. Reps should be prepared to answer "next step" questions such as:

"So if I'm interested, what happens next?"

"Would it be okay if I brought my mom in to take a look at it?"

"Where do we go from here?"

"What can I do to take this home?"

Recognizing the difference between mild interest and a desire to buy helps salespeople align their sales process to the buyer's journey. Rather than trying to force a sale when the customer is in the consideration stage or talking an eager prospect out of the purchase, you can time your responses to leading them to purchasing today. There are several small things that you can do throughout the process that help close your customers without saying a word.

First, when making calculations use a calculator. No mental math. No phonetically writing it down. Humans make mistakes. We all know that. Calculators don't. People are much more willing to believe numbers when they come from calculators. People will trust that calculators are telling the truth. When we do mental math or write it out on paper there is always an inkling of doubt that those are the right numbers. Eliminate the doubt and always use a calculator.

Secondly, know when to pull out paperwork. Paperwork triggers fear in customers the same way that a poisoned dart frog's color freaked out our ancestors. The reason for this is because paperwork means commitment. Makes people nervous. When do you traditionally see paperwork? When you feel that you are in a situation to pull out paperwork use clean and unwrinkled papers. You will look professional and confident. That professionalism and confidence is going to allow you to move your prospect into a position where they will sign on the dotted line and go from prospect to buyer.

CHAPTER 13: CUSTOMER SERVICE

Really good customer service will deliver sales. You are training salesmen to give the best possible advice and then to achieve the sale. People actually like you to ask for a sale because it shows you value their business.
John Caudwell

Giving good customer service needs to be at the top of your priority list. You must act like an independent company. You are in business for yourself. You can earn twice as much money if you discipline yourself every day to charge into work, get on top of what needs to be done, and stay on top.

Follow up Phone-Call
Call them the next day. Don't be chicken about it.

Follow up phone calls after a sale are immensely important. It kills buyers remorse and lets your customers relive the magical moment. Call to find out how it went, if they had given the gift yet and to let them know you have their back.

"I was calling to follow up on your last purchase. Have you given it yet?"

"Yes"

"I am so glad to hear it. You really made a great choice and I am thrilled that she loved it. It was a real pleasure getting to know you yesterday and we really appreciate you choosing us."

It is always worth it, and it is the easiest thing you can do. I dare say that 90% of the time it will be simple, easy and quick. They are going to appreciate your professionalism, concern and they may even be impressed. Even if on the rare occasion the customer had a negative experience then this becomes an opportunity to give exceptional customer service. You have already called them before they had to call you. That is customer service above and beyond anything most people experience.

Follow-up through phone calls and postcards is a good way to keep relationships strong. Another simple thing is asking customers, "Is there anything we're not doing we could be doing to serve you better?" Customers can give you tremendous insight into what you're doing right and what you need to work on. Studies have shown that more than two-thirds of consumers leave a store and don't return because they feel the retailer doesn't care about them, but only want to sell to them. Ask your customers what they want, what's important to them, and you'll know what you have to do to retain them.

Thank You Notes
Spoken thank you's are nice but written thank you's will never be forgotten. The rule to remember is, "Everyone gets a thank you card". Most companies will provide you with an unlimited number of thank you cards. Use them.

Small purchases and repairs will return to your store far more often than home run hitting buyers. If you send a thank you card to each of them, they will not only return for the smaller purchases, but they will request your help when it comes time for those slam dunk purchases.

Why do thank you cards make such a big impact? It is a sign of respect. The biggest excuse for not writing thank you cards is because it is a waste of time. As a jeweler you are essentially running your own business. You pay yourself through commissions and you are the one working with the customers. Thank you notes are one of your commitments to becoming an extraordinary jeweler and to personal growth.

How to Write a Thank You Card and When

When you write a thank you card show that you distinctly remember them. Show them that they are individuals to you, and not customers. Give a little detail in a part of the conversation that was meaningful to your customer. Once you remind them of your conversation say thank you and nothing more. Do not try to sell them in a thank you card. The second you do this it looks more like an ad and less like a personalized letter.

Nobody gets cards in this day and age. Only bills, supermarket ads and other things trying to get their money come through the mailbox. Someone out there was willing to put the thought of sending a genuine card in the mail to say congratulations on their anniversary. Don't try to get them to come in and buy, but let your name be on the front of their mind next time they decided to make a jewelry purchase.

When you write thank you cards correctly you will no longer be seen as a salesman You'll be seen as a friend who happens to know where the best deals are for jewelry. Customers attach loyalty to people, not just brands. Be the one who thanks them and develops an honest relationship with that person. It is more work, but the results will always pay off. Ask yourself, of these groups which is the easiest to sell?

1. Couples who walk in looking for engagement rings
2. Clients who come in after seeing one of your ads
3. Customers who come in because they know you, and who is happy with you and your services

It will be the third option every single time.

Client Book

Even when you close a sale and the customer is at the register you need to think big picture. Sure, you closed the sale today, but what about tomorrow? They will need more jewelry. Holidays are coming up and those holidays are more opportunities for you to help guide customers back into your store.

Keep in mind, you want quality over quantity. Not everyone will make the cut. Who can you sell over again even if it's a smaller purchase? Ever heard of the Pareto Principle? 80 percent of your sales comes from 20 percent of our efforts. Everyone deserves the best service but give extra attention to your 20%. A sale is a sale, even if the customer is difficult, but keep a record of those you can sell again.

The best way to do this is to keep a detailed customer profile that includes:

• The customer's name and complete contact information.
• Important dates such as the customer's birthday and anniversary.
• Names and personal dates for family members, and close friends.

- Preferences in metals, gems, colors, styles, and so forth.
- Key jewelry fittings like ring sizes and necklace and bracelet lengths.
- A complete purchase history, including dates, item descriptions, stock numbers, sketches or photos, amounts, and reasons for purchases.
- Items of interest shown but not yet purchased. (In other words, a wish list.)
- Bits of conversation that can help you remember them.

You will be surprised how incredibly easy it is to get this information. You can create your own customer profile sheets or print some from a free online source. All you have to do to fill them out is to place them in front of the customer. They will fill them out automatically. Do not fill it out yourself because it will feel like an interrogation to them. Sometimes they will be interested but do not want to buy that day. Get pertinent information by slapping that profile sheet in front of them.

Customer: "I will be back"

Jeweler: "Let me have you fill this out so that way when you come back and I am not here someone else will be able to pick up right where we left off"

Handing them a sheet with all the information is easier than asking them. Asking them when their anniversary is can be scary and feel like an interrogation after he just gave you his address, phone number and best time to reach him. By just handing him the sheet to feel out they will often go into robot mode and just fill out all the important information automatically. Organize all this information in a book. Look at it every day, every time you walk into work. See whose anniversary is coming up this next week, who has a birthday etc. Your book should be organized as follows:

1. Hot
2. Potentials
3. Interested

Use it to make more sales, better relationships and to give your customers better customer service. If you need to find out when to call them offer them a choice. Don't just ask when you can call. Ultimately, wardrobing and client development provide effective ways to create deeper and richer relationships with customers – and that's the true secret to success in the profession that you have chosen.

CHAPTER 14: REPAIRS AND CALLS

If you cannot do great things, do small things in a great way.
Napoleon Hill

The ace hidden under your sleeve when it comes to jewelry sales is your repair department. Repair services are one of the best ways to deliver OUTSTANDING customer service. Don't kid yourself, there is no jewelry repair sale in the world that can rival the excitement and thrill of selling a big juicy diamond. However, selling repairs is an important part of your job. You are here for all your customer's needs and keeping their already purchased jewelry in prime condition is an integral part of your relationship.

However, repair sales are often spit upon and abused. You need to take a good look deep down inside yourself and recognize your own personal attitude about selling repairs. What emotions do you feel when a customer comes in asking about your repair department? Do you give repairs the same amount of energy as you would a bridal up? Once you understand your honest take on repairs you can begin improving how it is you go about making repair sales.

The most important rule to remember when selling jewelry repair services is to never underestimate the value customers place on their broken jewelry. Jewelry purchases are romance purchases. Romance purchases create a long-lasting emotional attachment, and customers will have deep desires to have these items repaired, because they are more motivated by value and quality. In the vast majority of jewelry repair situations, price will not be the determining factor for your customers. People want a good value, but more importantly, and in most situations, they want quality.

Ask yourself, if you had a family heirloom and it needed to be repaired would you just get a quick patch job? Of course not, you would take it to the very best. When Grandma's ring is broken you never go to the discount stores, you go to someone who knows what it takes to fix it. They are looking for someone to trust and your store is where they chose to go. It is your duty to live up to their expectations and take the utmost care of their jewelry. You do that, you go above and beyond their expectations and you'll be doing more than making a jewelry repair customer happy. You will be leading that customer to giving you the trust to make their jewelry decisions and make many future sales with you. Naturally, trust is of paramount importance. Customers put their trust in jewelry stores with high levels of expertise and as many industry certifications as possible. That is why you, the jeweler extraordinaire, can also establish trust with jewelry customers through professional certification that reflects your knowledge, skill and commitment to professionalism. Would you look at that? You are ALREADY working on improving your knowledge! Look at you go.

There are certain pitfalls that you need to avoid so you

don't lose any of that trust. The first thing that will kill customer trust is if not inspecting every single ring you are handed. You need to uncover any repair work that every ring needs as soon as possible.

When selling jewelry repairs, take the time to get to know your customer and the history of the piece they need repaired. Don't just write up a tidy job card, give a customer a due date, and quickly say "goodbye," when he or she brings in the repair.

While your customer is in the store, give the piece a quick cleaning to give you time to get to know your customer and the piece's history. This information will provide you with valuable insights into how to sell jewelry repair services that best meets their needs and motivations. This is the time to take time to explain the jewelry repair process to the customer. Clear explanation and communication is vital to creating satisfied jewelry repair customers.

Demonstrating your knowledge and commitment to customer satisfaction by taking just a little extra time with a repair sale will reap tremendous rewards. To maximize your jewelry repair profits and close more repair sales, you must make the customer feel that their jewelry is important and that your store will give it the attention and care it deserves.

Once the piece is clean, take the time to carefully inspect it looking for any and all repair work that needs to be done. Your customer will be more likely to agree to the added costs of more comprehensive work if you take the time to put her needs and the needs of the piece first. People with the money to purchase such items can and will pay for expensive repairs when supplied with thorough explanations of the repair estimate.

What you can do to thoroughly explain how repairs happen there is a big secret that I am going to tell you that may change how you view repairs for the rest of your life.

Watch Your Jeweler

Front-line salespeople are often not bench experts. They don't know how jewelry is repaired and what it takes to keep jewelry in pristine condition. This isn't anything to be ashamed of. With a little effort, you can educate yourself by taking a trip to your jeweler's workbench. This is one of the most magical things that you can do to transform your attitude and knowledge regarding repairs. It allows you to actively describe how your repairs are done.

Lack of training is a major issue in jewelry stores when it comes to repairs. If you can tell someone on the spot what has to be done and how much it's going to cost, that's so much better than having to call them later and say, 'You know what? We were wrong about that cost.' That takes a toll on the relationship. And by having them miss that repair, you often leave a lot of money on the table. If you send someone away who came to get jewelry repaired, they're not going to buy jewelry with you the next time they're in the market for something.

Mistakes You Can't Have

Prepare yourself to give the best jewelry repair service as possible. Learn as much about your jewelry repairs as you can. There will be times when you stumble along the way but use those challenges to learn from them. However, there are mistakes that you cannot make.

You cannot make the price up in mid-air and speak it orally. People are apprehensive about what they hear and believe what they see. Have all prices written down so you can refer to the particular repair they request.

Whether it's a repair or a custom job, there's no real reason why you can't price it now. Besides, the customer will lose their enthusiasm if they feel like they must bargain or that they are simply paying that little extra you added on their repair to buy yourself a pizza later. Strike while the iron is hot. Stop wasting your time and theirs. Quote now. Quote Accurately. Quote Consistently.

Never, ever, ever, ever go and over-sell unnecessary repair work.

Whatever the situation, once you've lost a customer's trust, you've lost that customer forever.

What you should do, is under-promise and over-deliver.

What does that mean? That means that your average jewelry repair has a turnaround time of 3 days, but you tell your customer that their jewelry will be ready in a week. Imagine your customer's surprise when they get a call four days early telling them that their jewelry is done! Wouldn't you keep going back to the store where they are able to get your work done so quickly? If you say it will be done in three days and later you call them three days later, it won't seem as fast. Think of it like you are ordering something from Amazon. If your package comes in the day it says that is just what you expected, but when it comes a day early you get giddy with excitement.

Under-promising and over-delivering also gives you a cushion of safety. Say that your jeweler gets sick and can't work for two days. It is no biggie. You still have three extra days to over deliver to your customer. Always under-promise and over-deliver.

When it comes to repairs, savvy retailers don't sell the fix—they sell the restoration. Getting your customers to envision their finished piece, gleaming and reborn, is key to closing service tickets.

If a customer says, 'Wow, $125 is a lot to fix this ring,' you say, 'I know you think sizing this ring is simple, but we're going to do an excellent job with that repair; we're going to check and tighten every stone, guarantee our work for a year, and refinish the entire piece to make it look like the day your husband gave it to you. My jeweler's been doing this for 30 years. You do want that kind of expertise, don't you?'

Your customers want quality, and you can give them quality. Build that trust by knowing what you are doing, telling your customer what you are doing, and then under-promising and over-delivering. If there's trust between you and the customer, they'll almost always pay what you ask for.

Inbound Calls to Your Store

When someone calls into your store you should be jumping and prancing with joy. The inbound call is often the end-goal of massive multi-corporation marketing strategies and here's why—in many cases, by the time prospects make that call they are already far along the sales cycle and have tentatively decided to buy. When that phone rings, that means that you have already won.

You need to give them exactly what they are looking for. An informed, well trained professional who is going to give them the best deal. You can do this in a lot of ways. Take the following conversation for example.

phone rings

"Thank you for calling ABC jewelers this is my name,

how can I help you?"

"Hi, it says on your website that you do watch repair. How long does it take to replace a watch battery?"

"You actually called the best watch repair shop in the city. It will only take a couple of minutes and we will also give it a free polishing."

When the customer called in the jeweler didn't have to do anything special, just recited the usual greeting you hear when you call any jewelry store in the country. That is 100% ok. Fancy answers can freak people out. Calling is a scary thing that a lot of people actively try to avoid. It takes some courage to pick up a phone and call a total stranger. Keep opening lines simple and expected.

After the opening line your customers are going to jump right in and ask the question that is burning inside their minds. When they do, do two things:

1. Reassure them that they made the right choice
2. Offer them a deal/free service

In the above conversation you can see that using these two qualities is easy. First, they reassured them that they were the best when it came to the service that their customers needed. Then, the jeweler offered them a deal. Free watch polishing is not what they asked for, but now they are going to want it. Anyone can change their watch battery, but you are the only one who is going to go one step further and give them a deal right off the bat. Best part is, it doesn't cost you a thing! You are going to sell your watch repair at full price and your customer is going to feel like they are getting a deal. It is that easy.

CHAPTER 15: UNRULY CUSTOMERS

Aaararrgwwwh
Chewbacca

Sometimes you are going to be dealing with less than happy customers. So how do you handle those particular customers? The wrong way would be to rip their arms out of their sockets like a Wookie would do. The best thing to do is to look at the powerhouse of customer service and the home of the Wookies themselves; Disney.

Since it was founded in 1923, The Mouse house has captivated the masses by fostering imaginative, family friendly entertainment. Having grown into a $155 billion company today, Disney is also arguably the world's most successful diversified media conglomerate. Even that kind of success doesn't mean that everyone is going to be happy. Disney receives hundreds of thousands of complaints a year. However, even with all these complaints there is still a magical touch that brings millions to their doorstep every day. That isn't because they wave their magical wand and they magically disappear. They have taken on these complaints and are the champions of handling bad situations.

They do this by following a 5-step process to handle service failures, they call this the H.E.A.R.D technique. With this technique you'll be able to:

• Overcome customer concerns (to increase retention)

• Recover from customer service mistakes (to reduce churn and save valuable customer relationships)

• Explain complicated concepts simply (to reduce customer confusion and effort, which research suggests increases customer loyalty)

These steps are proven to ensure consistent service recovery every time. Since 1991 Disney has only lost revenue twice. I would take their advice if I was you.

(1) Hear

Whether it's face to face or over the phone, you should let your customers explain how they feel. Let them be heard with no interruptions. Give them the time to vent out their frustration first, after all these people are like us and they want someone to listen. Don't take it personally. Remember, the customer is not angry with you, they are displeased with the performance of your product or the quality of the service you provide. Your personal feelings are beside the point.

Listening patiently can defuse a situation, as long as the customer feels acknowledged in his or her complaint. Usually, this is the only step you need to take. Most problems that you face are very frequent and are easily correctable. When they are done talking, summarize what you've heard and ask any questions to further clarify their complaint. Body language can be critically important here. Keep eye contact. Stand or sit up straight. Keep your arms uncrossed. Show how closely you're paying attention to their problem.

You are the best person to hear this because you have the capability to make it right by them.

(2) Empathize
Show how genuinely you care about the customer's issue by validating them. Use phrases like "I understand how this must feel" or "I'd feel the same way too". Saying phrases like these shows how you understand their problem and will create a sense of trust.

(3) Apologize
Own the problem and be responsible by apologizing, this just might be what they're looking to hear. You can never make it right no matter how many times you apologize, but this step is as crucial as the resolution itself. A simple and sincere apology goes a long way. Whether the customer's complaint is legitimate or not is irrelevant. If you want her to stay a customer, you need to express an apology for the problem they are having (or perceive to be having). A simple, straightforward statement is often all that's needed: "I'm sorry you're not happy with our product. Let's see what we can do to make things right."

(4) Resolve
Do it and do it right! Make sure that you are empowered to make vital decisions in cases of failures. Asking the manager for approval can take time. Resolve the issue immediately if you can. Use phrases like "How can we make this right for you?" or "I'd be happy to resolve this for you right now." In most cases, that's all the customer is looking for—and may result in providing some degree of satisfaction.

(5) Diagnose
This is the most important part of the whole process. Making sure that the same issue won't happen again. There is where you should "Seek perfection, and settle for

excellence"—Disney Institute. Make sure that you analyze the issue and figure out why the failure occurred. Avoid blaming anyone for the problem and ensure that it won't happen again.

There is a six and final step that you should do after an intense customer.

(6) Take a Few Minutes on Your Own.

After the situation has been resolved and the customer is on her way, it's helpful for you to take your own "time-out." Even if you've handled the situation in the most professional way possible, it's still a stressful experience. Rather than let that stress linger inside you, take a short walk, treat yourself to a snack or find someone to talk to who makes you laugh. Then you'll be ready to once again engage with your customers. You can do that, can't you.

CHAPTER 16: SELLING CREDIT

Strive not to be a success, but rather to be of value.
Albert Einstein

Credit is a powerful tool that you can use to close sales. This isn't just because it benefits the customer because they can pay over a long period of time instead of one huge sum of money, but it benefits you just as much.

Benefits to you, the jeweler:
- More customers.
- They will return over and over.
- Increase of frequency of customer purchases
- Increase of average sale
- Increase of ad-ons

First and foremost, selling your customers on credit is going to keep them coming back to the store over and over. They are dedicated to your store. They have given you the time of day to sit down and fill out those credit applications, and they don't want to have to do it anywhere else. Not only that, but they will come back more often.

Offering credit also expands the budget of your

customer allowing them to buy bigger, better, representations of their love. Not into bigger and better? Well then maybe give them a necklace to go with their ring as a just because I love you present. It is much easier for add-ons because instead of adding hundreds of dollars that they need to spend today; they are just adding $5 to their monthly payment. Don't you think that $5 is a fantastic deal for a diamond of any type?

This is not only a huge benefit to you, but also to your customer. Credit allows customers to fulfill their dreams. Pinterest is full of fun, delightful rings that are so easy to become obsessed about, however some budgets don't allow for people to get their dream ring. Credit is the unsung hero because you take their budget and you are literally enlarging it. They can now afford bigger than their dreams.

Secondly its flexible. The world we live in is full of ups and downs. Lines of credit are not supposed to weigh you down, they help lift you up. Now instead of taking out a huge chunk of your savings, you can take little bits out a weekly paycheck and keep your savings stockpiled for a rainy day. Not only that, but your credit score is going to improve. That means that using credit for a jewelry purchase instead of cash will help newlyweds afford better houses and more seasoned couples afford better toys.

With so many benefits surrounding credit, you have to offer it to every customer. You will close more deals and establish long lasting relationships with customers that will come back to you again and again. So how do you use your financing options to close the deals? I've broken it down into four easy tips.

#1 Bring up Financing Early.
One of the biggest mistakes a sales rep makes is waiting

until the end of the sales process or waiting for the customer to ask if you offer financing. You are wasting time by not bringing it up early and may even discover whether or not your customer can qualify or if they don't have the cash to pay for it.

#2 Memorize the 24 Month or 2-Year Factor

Knowing this will help you ballpark a payment and get a reaction from the customer to your pricing and affordability. Read the body language and then adjust as needed. You can increase or decrease the term from there to make the affordability fit the customer's rationale. There is a huge difference between hearing this ring costs $4,000 and one that only costs $100 a month. Depending on how much you put down, it could even be less. $100 a month sounds much more reasonable that. Plus, it is suddenly much more affordable. They can handle a $100 a month. That's easy.

#3 Get a Completed Credit App Before Leaving

This shows a level of commitment from the customer and increases the level of which they intend to do business with you!

#4 Avoid Surprises

Ask this one question to avoid any surprises. You need to ask the heart to heart questions to gauge your chances of closing the sale. The one simple question pertaining to financing is, "Are there any problems with your credit history that I need to know about or prep the finance company for ahead of time?" You may be surprised at the feedback you get. Going in with "eyes wide open" is another way of helping you determine if this is a tire-kicker or buyer. If you hear them say, "Well we did have a bankruptcy a couple years ago," it helps set the stage for what may be the end result or determine other avenues to get funding.

CHAPTER 17: TAKEAWAY

Champions are not the ones who always win races - champions are the ones who get out there and try. And try harder the next time. And even harder the next time. 'Champion' is a state of mind. They are devoted. They compete to best themselves as much if not more than they compete to best others.
Simon Sinek

This may be the final chapter, but it is not the end. This is the beginning. You now have the fundamentals, skills, and knowledge necessary to not only make enough commission to pay for this book a hundred times over, but to change the way you approach customers from here on out.

Success comes to those who chase it. It is something that you have to choose for yourself. The path you have chosen is not easy. It will beat you down and keep you there if you allow it to. It can suck the energy from your soul or breathe life into you like you have never before experienced.

You have chosen to be successful. You have chosen to go and take the punches. You punch back. You fight to become better and you are well on your way to becoming a champion in the octagon of sales. The first punch you need to throw is going to be setting goals for yourself.

Take the following couple of pages to write down your goals. Write down a goal that you are going to accomplish this week. Write down a goal that you are going to accomplish in a month. Finally, write down a goal that you want to accomplish in a year. Most importantly. Every day write down your goal for the day. Be different. Be better. And most importantly, make them feel special. You got this.

WRITE YOUR GOALS BELOW:

BONUS CHAPTER: VOCABULARY

Two roads diverged in a wood, and I—I took the one less traveled by, And that has made all the difference.
Robert Frost

You are a jeweler, so start talking like a jeweler. Three words you used to much: beautiful, pretty, lovely. Let's expand that vocabulary. We can make our products much more engaging, entertaining, and effective. We want to to feel emotion. "Beautiful" is so vague and obvious. That means you need to know more words than just sparkle and love. Here is a compilation of words that you should add to your selling vocabulary. Glance through these on occasion to keep your presentations crisp.

adjustable
adorable
alluring
antique
artisan
artisanal
attention-getting
beautiful
bejeweled
bold
brilliant
carved
casual
cathedral
certified
charming
chic
classic
comfortable
comfy
compelling
complex
contemporary
cool
coordinating
cutting-edge
dainty
dapper
decorative
delicate
dependable
designer
detailed
distinctive
dramatic
durable
easy-to-maintain

eco-friendly
edgy
elegant
encased
engineered
engraved
etched
ethnic
everyday
exceptional
exciting
exotic
expensive-looking
exquisite
eye-catching
faceted
fancy
fashion-forward
feminine
finely detailed
flattering
flawless
flexible
flirty
floral
funky
genuine
glamorous
glittering
glitzy
gold-toned
gorgeous
graceful
half-priced
hand-carved
hand-finished
hand-wrapped

handcrafted
handmade
hassle-free
heirloom-quality
high-class
high-performance
hott
hypoallergenic
imported
inlaid
innovative
intricate
iridescent
jewel-tone
keepsake
latest
lightweight
long-lasting
lovely
luscious
luxurious
marbled
masculine
metallic
minimalist
modern
mosaic
never-before-seen
one-of-a-kind
opaque
original
ornate
piercing
precious
precise
premium
prismatic

professional
queenly
radiant
reliable
rocker-style
rugged
sale-priced
sassy
scratch-resistant
sexy
shimmering
simple
sleek
slender
slip-on
smokey
smooth
snag-free
solid
sophisticated
sporty
streamlined
striking
studded
stunning
stylish
subtle
superior
supportive
suspended
tantalizing
tapered
teardrop
textured
timeless
tiny
top-of-the-line

ADORNMENT

trendsetting
tribal
two-tone
unique
versatile
vintage
wardrobe-friendly
water-resistant
waterproof
wear-anywhere
whimsical
wrapped.

ABOUT THE AUTHOR

Carson is currently working on his triple major in International Business, Finance and Economics at Utah State University. In 2015 he left his family to be a volunteer in Russia where he fell in love with the Russian language. During that time his favorite memory was getting his own private "blueberry bar" on a flight to Finland. After his time abroad, Carson jumped into the jewelry world and became obsessed with jewelry sales. For three years he studied techniques, fundamentals and sales practices from great salesmen across North America. Adornment is the culmination of his experiences and he wishes to share them with the world.